Cambridge Studies in Social Anthropology

General Editor: Jack Goody

54

ON ANTHROPOLOGICAL KNOWLEDGE

This book is published as part of the joint publishing agreement established in 1977 between the Fondation de la Maison des Sciences de l'Homme and the Press Syndicate of the University of Cambridge. Titles published under this arrangement may appear in any European language or, in the case of volumes of collected essays, in several languages.

New books will appear either as individual titles or in one of the series which the Maison des Sciences de l'Homme and the Cambridge University Press have jointly agreed to publish. All books published jointly by the Maison des Sciences del l'Homme and the Cambridge University Press will be distributed by the Press throughout the world.

Cet ouvrage est publié dans le cadre de l'accord de co-édition passé en 1977 entre la Fondation de la Maison des Sciences de l'Homme et le Press Syndicate de l'Université de Cambridge. Toutes les langues européennes sont admises pour les titres couverts par cet accord, et les ouvrages collectifs peuvent paraître en plusieurs langues.

Les ouvrages paraissent soit isolément, soit dans l'une des séries que la Maison des Sciences de l'Homme et Cambridge University Press ont convenu de publier ensemble. La distribution dans le monde entier des titres ainsi publiés conjointement par les deux établissements est assurée par Cambridge University Press.

For other titles in the Cambridge Studies in Social Anthropology series, turn to page 109.

On anthropological knowledge

Three essays

DAN SPERBER

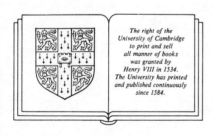

The right of the
University of Cambridge
to print and sell
all manner of books
was granted by
Henry VIII in 1534.
The University has printed
and published continuously
since 1584.

Cambridge University Press

Cambridge
New York   Port Chester   Melbourne   Sydney

& Editions de la Maison des Sciences de l'Homme

Paris

Published by the Press Syndicate of the University of Cambridge
The Pitt Building, Trumpington Street, Cambridge CB2 1RP
40 West 20th Street, New York, NY 10011, USA
10 Stamford Road, Oakleigh, Melbourne 3166, Australia

Originally published in French as *Le Savoir des Anthropologues* by HERMANN, éditeurs
des sciences et des arts, Paris, 1982 and © Hermann, 1982

First published in English, with revisions, by the Cambridge University Press and the
Maison des Sciences de l'Homme as *On Anthropological Knowledge*

English version © Maison des Sciences de l'Homme and Cambridge University Press 1985
Reprinted 1987, 1989

Printed in the United States of America

Library of Congress Cataloging in Publication Data

Sperber, Dan.
On anthropological knowledge.
(Cambridge studies in social anthropology; no. 54)
Translation of: Le savoir des anthropologues.
Includes index.
1. Ethnology – Philosophy – Addresses, essays, lectures.
2. Irrationalism (Philosophy) – Addresses, essays,
lectures.   3.   Lévi-Strauss, Claude – Addresses, essays,
lectures.   I.   Title.   II.   Series.
GN345.S6313   1985   306   84-21481

ISBN 0-521-26748-X hard covers
ISBN 0-521-31851-3 paperback

Contents

ON ANTHROPOLOGICAL KNOWLEDGE

Introduction

What is anthropology? A philosophical tradition going back to classical antiquity, an academic discipline established in the nineteenth century, a method developed in the last few decades.

The Sophist Protagoras claimed that his teaching would make good citizens. Socrates wondered: can virtue really be taught? Is it, we would ask today, innate or acquired? Protagoras first answered by means of a fable. The gods, having shaped the mortal species, gave Prometheus and Epimetheus the job of dividing all desirable qualities among these species. Epimetheus took charge. He gave each species the means to survive: to some he gave strength, to others speed; to some he gave claws or horns, to others wings to flee or underground shelters to hide. He protected them against the weather by means of hides, furs, and hooves. To each species he assigned its own food. He made some species carnivorous, and endowed their prey with great fecundity.

Alas Epimetheus – whose very name evokes lack of foresight – forgot the human species. Prometheus arrived too late: while all other animals were well provided for, man stood naked and defenseless. In desperation, Prometheus stole from the gods fire and crafts and gave them to man. Thereafter, humans honored the gods, acquired speech, and learned to build houses, make clothes, and till the soil. But they were scattered on the surface of the earth and were prey to wild beasts. They still lacked the political skills required to form cities. Zeus, eager to ensure the survival of the species, ordered Hermes to give all humans the necessary sense of respect and justice.

Protagoras's fable nicely exposes a paradox which, since the Sophists, has been at the core of Western anthropological thought:[1] humans are, by nature, deprived of natural qualities. Other animals are naturally equipped to survive. Humans owe their survival to empirical, technical, and moral knowledge which they acquire progressively. Other animals live naturally in what we would call today an ecological equilibrium. It is

1

by becoming civilized that humans, for their part, adapt to their natural environment and establish harmonious mutual relationships.

If virtue may appear to be natural, if it may seem to Socrates that there are no teachers of virtue, it is, on the contrary, argues Protagoras, because everybody helps to teach it: "just as if you were looking for a teacher of Greek, you wouldn't find one" (Plato, *Protagoras*, 328a). In this respect, language and virtue which are transmitted by society as a whole, contrast with arts and crafts which have appointed masters. It is, however, not a contrast between nature and culture, but one between shared culture and special knowledge. Today's anthropologists echo Protagoras when they insist: "everything is cultural."

What are the common and specific attributes of humans? This question, central to anthropology, can only be answered in a speculative fashion. Human languages, cultures, and social systems are specific to the species, but they are not universally shared: they are, on the contrary, the main source of differences among humans. If humans share specific attributes beyond anatomy, these must be the mental capacities which make possible the development of a variety of languages, cultures, and social systems. But what are these capacities? This has been the central issue of philosophical anthropology. For empiricists such as Locke, these capacities amount to an indefinite malleability and receptiveness, so that knowledge owes all its content and structure to experience and to the environment. For rationalists such as Kant, human cognitive capacities comprise innate categories and principles which structure human knowledge and limit its variability.

From the fifteenth century onwards, the rediscovery of Classical Antiquity and the discoveries of the great travelers brought about a much greater awareness of the diversity of cultures. Philosophers however showed limited interest. In 1799, a *Society of Observers of Man* was founded in Paris. Although short-lived, it foreshadowed modern anthropological associations. Joseph-Marie Degérando contributed some "Considerations on the Diverse Methods to be Followed in the Observation of Savage Peoples"[2] in which he pointed out, not without reason, that "philosophers spent time in vain disputes in their schools about the nature of man, instead of uniting to study him in the area of the universe" (Degérando, 1969: 65).

It took until the middle of the nineteenth century for philosophical anthropology to give birth to two well-established empirical disciplines, with their chairs, their associations and their journals: psychology, which studies mental capacities through their manifestations in individual behavior, and anthropology, in a new and more restricted sense of the term, which aims to throw light on what humans are by studying who they are. The new anthropology had two main branches: physical anthropology, partly discredited since because of the racist and eugenist theories that developed within it (but, thanks to advances in biology, it has now taken a new start), and cultural anthropology, which has become so prominent that it is commonly referred to as simply "anthropology."[3]

Cultures are the collective output of human mental abilities. In principle, then, cultural anthropology and psychology should have a close and fruitful relationship. They deal with different outputs of the same general device: the human mind. This was self-evident for people such as Wilhelm Wundt and Edward Tylor. Wundt, the founder of experimental psychology, also wrote a ten-volume anthropological treatise. Tylor, often considered the founder of modern cultural anthropology, was guilty, in the eyes of his successors, of the sin of "psychologicism." Actually, the two disciplines soon parted company. They did so on theoretical and on methodological grounds.

Anthropology and psychology developed in an empiricist atmosphere which they themselves helped perpetuate. From an empiricist point of view, the study of mental mechanisms sheds no light on the content of cultures: the mental malleability of humans is thought to be so great as to allow cultures to vary without any constraint other than those imposed by the social or natural environment. Conversely, the study of cultures sheds no light on mental mechanisms apart from the fact that their diversity is taken to illustrate the malleability of the human mind. For a psychology and an anthropology sharing such empiricist foundations, there was little left to do in common. After Tylor and until Lévi-Strauss, anthropologists showed little interest in the psychology of the intellect. Some of them, Malinowski or Ruth Benedict for instance, did pay attention to the psychology of emotions, which had hardly been touched by the debate between empiricism and rationalism and which had benefited from the contribution of psychoanalysis.

Today, most anthropologists acknowledge the legacy of Durkheim, Max Weber, or Marx rather than that of William James, Wundt, or Freud, and going further back, that of Hobbes or Montesquieu rather than that of Hume or Kant. Such acknowledgments are beyond dispute: in matters of intellectual filiation, it behooves the descendants to appoint their ancestors. By the same token, it is not inconceivable that the next generation of anthropologists will take its inspiration from psychology rather than from sociology, from the philosophy of mind rather than from the philosophy of law. It is not absurd either to hope that, rather than having a mere reversal of allegiances, a fruitful balance might be struck between the two traditions.

The split between psychology and anthropology is not only due to a theoretical bias, but also, and perhaps more importantly, to a primacy given to methodological issues. Most experimental psychologists have acknowledged as psychological only facts and assumptions that come out of laboratory experiments. Most anthropologists have been exclusively concerned with problems encountered in collecting, presenting, and classifying cultural data: "anthropology" for them is just a better sounding synonym of "ethnography."

Bronislaw Malinowski, a young Polish anthropologist living in Britain, happened to be visiting Australia when the First World War broke out. Because he was an Austrian subject, and therefore, technically, an enemy, he was forbidden to go back to Europe till the end of the war. He took advantage of this forced exile to study the inhabitants of the Trobriand Islands. For two years, he set his tent in their midst, learned their language, participated as much as he could in their daily life, expeditions, and festivals, and took everything down in his notebooks. In 1922, he published *Argonauts of the Western Pacific*, which became a model for ethnography and which still is, in spite of criticisms and revisions, one of its masterpieces.

Actually, well before Malinowski, missionaries and colonial officers lived for long periods of time among faraway peoples and learned their language. Some of the descriptions they published are of a quality and wealth of detail not always matched by today's professionals. Among anthropologists themselves, Morgan, Boas, Rivers and others already had done fieldwork in the nineteenth century. What was new, however, with Malinowski, was the ideal he set himself: to move away from other Europeans, to live among the natives with no other purpose than that of getting to know them, to observe social life by participating in it as intimately as possible and as long as necessary, to study its every aspect however trivial, to collect every kind of data on every kind of occasion, and, most important of all, to try and grasp the natives' point of view, to understand *their* vision of *their* world.[4]

In the foreword of *Argonauts*, Malinowski worried: "Ethnology is in the sadly ludicrous, not to say tragic, position, that at the very moment when it begins to put its workshop in order, to forge its proper tools, to start ready for work on its appointed task, the material of its study melts with hopeless rapidity." Sixty years later, we see that Malinowski was wrong in thinking that the cultures studied by anthropologists were about to vanish. He was right however in fearing that the kind of study he proposed could not be pursued much longer. His methodological ideal presupposed an ideal object: a small homogeneous society, nearly closed to external influences, but one which the anthropologist could penetrate in order to become, through patience and humility, its proud interpreter. Did such an ideal object ever exist? Human societies are less homogeneous and more open to one another, better able to survive intrusions than is generally assumed. Like regions in geography or periods in history,

4

they are not well-bounded objects that can be taken in isolation and exhaustively studied. Colonizers rather than anthropologists were the first to develop the picture of continents peopled by a mosaic of primitive tribes, fast with arrows, but slow to exchange ideas, and open by their very inferiority to European intervention. That picture did not long out-live colonization itself.

It is, today, the normative rather than descriptive idea of a nation-state that inspires militants and politicians of former colonies. Nationalism is a Western-born idea, but one which has been turned against the West. In the same way, the influence of modern industrial society on the re-mainder of the world has been steadily growing, but it has not been passively accepted. Traditional cultures have changed, they have not dis-solved. The part, however small, that anthropologists have played in this process of transformation has been criticized. When they are not sus-pected of political wrongdoing or of spying, anthropologists are accused of belated tribalism and of having multiplied ethnic stereotypes while claiming to replace them with a scientific knowledge of peoples.

The posthumous publication, in 1967, of Malinowski's field diary caused a scandal: the master's passions had not been so virtuous; he had been obsessed with ambition, tormented by affective and sexual loneli-ness; worse still, he had preferred the landscapes of the Western Pacific to its inhabitants, of whom he sometimes spoke with an exasperation tinged with racism. This scandal brought out some of the delusions be-hind anthropology's self-image. But more significant is today's cry from the heart of a Trobriand Islander, John Kasaipwalova. Having too often heard: "Ah! The Trobriand Islands! Malinowski! Free love!," he warns: "If we are going to depend on anthropological studies to define our history and our culture and our 'future', then we are *lost!*" (quoted in Young, 1979: 17).

Need one say it? Anthropologists have neither the authority nor the competence to act as spokesmen for the people who have tolerated their presence, and even less to give the world professional guidance in moral or political matters. Anthropologists are ordinary women and men. Yet the experience that a few hundreds of them will have gone through is an extraordinary one. Only for a few tormented decades of human history, will such an experience have been possible. What knowledge do anthro-pologists draw from their fieldwork experience? How do they succeed in conveying it? What general problems does this knowledge solve or raise? Such are the questions I want to address.

The knowledge an anthropologist acquires in the field takes on two forms: documents and intuitions. In his trunks, the anthropologist brings back a field diary, linguistic files, an herbarium, maps, sketches, photo-graphs, tapes, genealogies, interview protocols, and notebooks filled with remarks scribbled on his knees in the darkness of a smoky hut, or leaning against a tree in the forest, or in the evening, alone at last, under the light of a petrol lamp. These documents are about men, women, children, households, neighborhoods, villages, fields, labors, crafts, food, plants, animals, markets, festivals, sacrifices, diviners' consultations, crises of spirit possession, conflicts, murders, vengeance, funerals, meetings, chiefs, ancestors, songs, dreams, and the reason why snakes have no legs.

For the anthropologist, these sundry documents are the products and the traces of a coherent experience: Over time the society became more familiar, he learned what was expected from him, what to expect from others, he could anticipate how many of his queries would be answered, he became sensitive to the humor or the sternness of a remark, to the friendliness or the coldness of a gesture, he laughed and he cried with his hosts. Anthropologists develop an intuitive knowledge which allows them to understand the documents they have collected and to relate them to one another. But how are they to share this understanding?

It is, in any case, quite a challenge to try and condense in a book, which will be read in a few hours, the experience of several years, an experience, moreover, without parallel in the life of most readers. Anthropologists compound this initial difficulty when they demand that their ethnographic writings not only give an account of their field experience, but also serve as the basis of a comparative and general anthropology. In order to achieve both ends at the same time, most anthropologists write in an intermediate style, leaving little space either for raw documents or for theoretical speculation. The culture under study is displayed in the form of a continuous and homogeneous discourse, neither too concrete, nor too abstract, and organized in chapters of equal length. Works of the same school often have the same table of contents, in order, no doubt, to pave the way for the work of comparison, which is always planned but rarely undertaken. With few exceptions, to read these writings requires a commendable perseverance.

Between what anthropologists have learned and what they manage to convey, great is the loss of knowledge. The intense experience of field-work turns into a painstaking disquisition. Voices merge, losing their timber and intonation. Individuals become mere representatives of their groups. The same anthropological jargon serves equally well – or equally badly – to describe the institutions and to render the ideas of the Bororo of Brazil, the Nuer of Sudan, or the Trobriand Islanders. A conformist anthropologist (if there is such a person in this highly individualistic profession) might explain: "Such is the price to pay in order to convert field experience into scientific data." The heretic would retort: "Well then, the price has been paid; but where are the goods? Has anthropological field-work much improved our knowledge of human nature?"

Introduction

The Conformist We have a better knowledge of human beings and we see that they are governed by their cultures, and not by their nature.

The Heretic Protagoras already said so much.

The Conformist Maybe he did, but all he could offer was speculation. Anthropologists offer evidence. Evidence which shows that no idea is innate, no behavior is natural.

The Heretic Is the evidence quite conclusive? Couldn't one object that . . .

The Conformist Yes, it is conclusive. Anyhow, it is no longer the aim of anthropological theory to describe a so-called human nature; its aim is to understand how cultures and societies are structured, and how they change. Would you dispute that our understanding of these matters has improved? It has, thanks to anthropological fieldwork.

The Heretic But was it necessary that the least academic form of research should yield the most academic form of literature?

The Conformist Academic, *Tristes Tropiques*? Academic, *The Children of Sanchez*? And I could mention several other titles. I'll grant you, though, that few anthropological works are read for pleasure. Nor is it their purpose. When anthropologists describe a ritual, or a kinship system, their aim is not to please, it is to explain. Theirs is not a literary task, but a scientific one.

The Heretic Scientific, really? Isn't that wishful thinking? A theory is scientific when it is neither trivially true, nor manifestly false, when its scope is too large to allow verification by an examination of all the relevant instances, and when its import is precise enough to determine in advance what would count as counter-evidence. Are there, in your anthropology, theories which meet these criteria?

The Conformist You are confusing "sciences" and "natural sciences." Anthropology is a social science. When human beings study human beings, they are able not only to observe them as a naturalist would, they are able also, and more importantly, to understand the people they observe by communicating with them. As a result, the social sciences have access to data of an unparalleled wealth and relevance, without counterpart in the natural sciences, even though the exploitation of these data might not lead to rigorously testable theories.

Let the conformist have the last word here; it is the heretic who will express himself in the remainder of the book.

The three essays collected in the present volume can be read independently of one another, but they have been written with a single purpose: to offer constructive criticism of the way ethnography is written and anthropological theory is developed. Taken together, these essays should help outline an epistemology of anthropology, a discipline which imposes on its practitioners great personal demands, only a loose methodology, and no theoretical standards whatsoever.

In the first essay, "Interpretive Ethnography and Theoretical Anthropology," I try to show how literary practices and scientific ambitions hamper each other in anthropology. I argue that ethnography aims at interpretation and anthropology at explanation; in order better to achieve these aims, and to entertain more fruitful relationships, the two disciplines should first free themselves from one another. (This essay, entirely

7

rewritten for the present volume, develops and modifies the substance of my paper "L'interprétation en anthropologie," in *L'Homme*, 1981, XXI, 1, itself a revision of a paper presented at Florence in 1978 at the conference on "Levels of Reality" organized by Massimo Piatelli-Palmarini and sponsored by the Fondation Royaumont.)

"Cultural relativism" is the most general and the most generally accepted theory in anthropology. It has two aspects, a moral and a cognitive one. According to moral relativism, there are no moral values shared by all humans; according to cognitive relativism, there is no reality shared by all humans. In the second essay of this volume, "Apparently Irrational Beliefs," I challenge the arguments used in favor of cognitive relativism, particularly the seemingly decisive argument provided by the diversity of human beliefs. I propose a rationalist solution to the problem raised by this diversity. I also evoke the troubles I once had with a dragon. (This essay is a revised and expanded version of a paper by the same title published in *Rationality and Relativism*, Martin Hollis and Steven Lukes eds., Oxford, Blackwell, 1982.)

My purpose, in "Claude Lévi-Strauss Today," the third essay in this volume, was neither to attack, nor to defend the most ambitious work in modern anthropology. In presenting the work of Claude Lévi-Strauss in a didactic yet unorthodox fashion, I have tried, rather, to illustrate the difficulties, the doubts, and the glimmers of hope that are part of any theoretical undertaking in anthropology. (This essay is a revised and expanded version of a paper entitled "Claude Lévi-Strauss" published in *Structuralism and Since*, John Sturrock ed., Oxford, Oxford University Press, 1979.)

This book was first published in French under the title *Le Savoir des Anthropologues* (Paris, Hermann, 1982). In preparing the English version I have made a number of substantive revisions and additions, particularly in chapters one and two.

I wish to thank Scott Atran, Pierre Berès, Pascal Boyer, Catherine Cullen, Jeanne Favret-Saada, Lawrence Hirshfeld, Martin Hollis, Donald Levine, Steven Lukes, Judith Olmstead, Massimo Piatelli-Palmarini, Pierre Smith, Jenka and Manès Sperber, John Sturrock, Tzvetan Todorov, and Deirdre Wilson who, through their encouragement and criticisms, have helped me give their final form to these essays. I wish to mention also the names of two anthropologists who have had no direct role in this work, but whose indirect role is considerable: Georges Balandier's seminars at the Sorbonne taught me how to read anthropological works critically; Rodney Needham's tutorials at Oxford helped me become aware of some of the main problems in the discipline, the very problems discussed in this book. In reflecting on anthropological knowledge, I had in mind the teaching of Georges Balandier and of Rodney Needham. To both of them, I am deeply grateful.

1
Interpretive ethnography and theoretical anthropology

Are social sciences really scientific? Are they like natural sciences? Anthropologists have joined in this philosophical debate. According to A. R. Radcliffe-Brown, for instance, whose simple ideas were for a time accepted as dogma, anthropology was to become a "natural science of society." The only obstacles to such a development were prejudices to overcome and habits to modify.[1] Radcliffe-Brown's successor at Oxford, E. E. Evans-Pritchard, argued on the contrary that anthropology belonged to the humanities, not to the sciences:

It studies societies as moral systems and not as natural systems . . . , it is interested in design rather than in process, and . . . it therefore seeks patterns and not scientific laws, and interprets rather than explains (Evans-Pritchard 1962: 26).

Neither of these two views of anthropology succeeded in gaining general acceptance. The project of a scientific anthropology meets with a major difficulty: it is impossible to describe a cultural phenomenon, an election, a mass, or a football game for instance, without taking into account the ideas of the participants. However, ideas cannot be observed, but only intuitively understood; they cannot be described but only interpreted. Thus the description of cultural phenomena raises epistemological issues without counterpart in the natural sciences. Radcliffe-Brown and his followers chose to ignore these issues, which reduces their optimism regarding the scientific future of anthropology to a mere act of faith. The pessimism of Evans-Pritchard is more in keeping with the actual practice of anthropologists, but it ignores their proclaimed desire to arrive at scientifically respectable generalizations.

There is, nowadays, a growing support for a third view of anthropology: though it is closer to that of Evans-Pritchard than to that of Radcliffe-Brown, it takes into account not only what anthropologists actually do, but also what they hope ultimately to achieve. Clifford Geertz, the foremost proponent of this view of anthropology, drawing both on hermeneutics in the tradition of Dilthey, and on modern semiotics, argues that the right, or even the only way to *describe* cultural phenomena is,

9

precisely, to *interpret* them[2]. Why should this be the case? Because cultural phenomena are vehicles of meaning, they are signs, messages, texts – "the culture of a people," he writes, "is an ensemble of texts" (Geertz 1973: 452) – and because interpretation is a particular form of description, the form required to describe such facts of meaning. Thus anthropology *is* a science, but a science of a particular type: it is an interpretive science. Like any other science, anthropology aims at an objective and general knowledge. However, the special character of the descriptions it uses makes it somewhat less ambitious in this respect than the natural sciences.

Is it possible, though, to reduce cultural phenomena to signs, and culture to a system of meanings? In *Rethinking Symbolism*, I explained at length why I believe that such a reduction is unwarranted. If "meaning" is understood in a loose sense, then everything and anything has meaning: dark clouds *mean* that it will rain. To have meaning in that sense is not characteristic of cultural phenomena, and hence is not relevant here. If "meaning" is understood in a more precise way, as, say, in linguistics, then phenomena of meaning pervade culture, but they are not alone: they are interwoven with, for instance, ecological phenomena, or with psychological phenomena of a different type. The picture of anthropologists applying to "texts" the type of description they require, however attractive it may be, is a misleading one.

I propose to develop a fourth view of anthropological knowledge. I shall suggest that the interpretive practice of anthropologists and their scientific ambitions might be reconciled, but not without a prior divorce. Today, the label "anthropology" covers two quite different disciplines which were in no way predestined for a monogamous union: interpretive ethnography, a lively and somewhat troubled discipline, and anthropology properly speaking, which consists of little more than a vague scientific project nursed in a compost of philosophical reminiscences.

Most anthropologists would be better – and no less honorably – described as ethnographers. They are more interested in specific cultures than in Homo sapiens's cultural abilities and dispositions, in varieties of human experience than in its variability. Ethnography is an important pursuit in its own right. It answers a legitimate curiosity as to what it is like to belong to another culture, to be Nuer, Tibetan, or French – a curiosity which is not so much about facts as about the way these facts are subjectively experienced, and which calls for interpretations rather than mere descriptions.

The task of theoretical anthropology, on the other hand, is to account for the variability of human cultures. Like any other science, it must answer the question: what is empirically possible? And hence: what is empirically impossible? Like any other science, anthropology requires data, that is descriptions of the real world (the real world being a particular case of an empirically possible world, with the extra advantage of being observable). An accumulation of data, however, does not make a science. When does data contribute to science? When it is reliable and relevant enough to constitute evidence for or against some general and non-trivial hypotheses.

It might seem, then, that the huge mass of data collected by ethnographers is twice devoid of scientific usefulness: today, because there are hardly any anthropological hypotheses to confirm or disconfirm; forever, because the interpretive character of these data is not compatible with the required level of reliability. Yet, without ethnographic evidence, no science of culture is conceivable.

Can this fundamental obstacle to the development of a scientific anthropology be overcome? Can the apparent antinomy between an interpretive and a descriptive approach be resolved? I shall argue that interpretations can constitute scientific data, but on one condition: they must be accompanied by a "descriptive comment." In current ethnography, however, this condition is not fulfilled; it is not even understood. This failure may be of little consequence for ethnography as such, but it hampers the development of anthropology proper and forbids a fruitful relationship between the two disciplines.

Interpretation and description

Interpretations and descriptions are *representations*, just like reproductions, scale models, quotations, translations, explanations, theories, and memories. A representation is a thing, physical or mental, which, for some intellectual purposes, can replace ("stand for") the object it represents. When subjects perceive, understand, or enjoy a representation, it is, to a certain extent, as if they were perceiving, understanding or enjoying the object represented itself. To play such a role, a representation must be *adequate* to its object. There are many types of representational adequacy: a scale model and an explanation, for instance, are not adequate in the same way. In order to characterize some particular type of representation, one must first say under what conditions is such a representation adequate.

Among representations, descriptions have a special place. A *description* is a representation which is adequate when it is true. Truth-or-falsity is an exclusive property of propositions. Only utterances convey propositions. Hence descriptions have to be in the form of utterances. The counterpart of this constraint is that descriptions can serve as premises or be derived as conclusions in a logical argument. They may imply or contradict one another. Thus they can be used to confirm or disconfirm one another, and, in particular, to confirm or disconfirm explanations (which are descriptions too, but of a more abstract and usually more speculative kind). These properties make descriptions uniquely open to systematic evaluation and to use as scientific evidence. Other representations, whatever their specific merits, cannot directly be exploited in the same way.

There are, it seems, two large categories of non-descriptive representations: reproductions on the one hand, and interpretations on the other. Reproductions and interpretations can be used as scientific evidence only indirectly and to the extent that their relationship to reality can itself be properly described. A non-descriptive representation needs what I propose to call a *descriptive comment*. A descriptive comment identifies the object represented and specifies the type of representation involved. It thereby makes it possible to draw empirical inferences from a non-descriptive representation. It provides, so to speak, the directions for its use. Trivial examples of descriptive comments are captions of pictures, headings of diagrams, or legends of maps. The legend of a map makes it possible to infer, say, from the presence of a dark patch on the right side of the map, the existence of a forest in the eastern part of the area represented.

The descriptive comment of a pictorial representation, being verbal material, stands apart. It is sometimes hard, on the other hand, to distinguish the descriptive comment from the representation commented on when *both* are verbal. Descriptions are not the only representations in verbal form. So also are quotations (which belong to the category of reproductions) or summaries (which belong to the category of interpretations). These non-descriptive verbal representations combine with their descriptive comments and form complex utterances: generally, the representation proper is put in a subordinate clause or in quotation marks; the comment forms a main clause and specifies what is being represented, and how. This is the case, for instance, when somebody's words are reported in the direct or in the indirect style, with an accompanying main clause comment which names the speaker and describes the circumstances.

A *reproduction* (for instance a quotation, or a scale model) is a representation which is adequate to the extent that it physically resembles that which it represents. The adequacy of a reproduction can never be absolute. On the other hand it is relatively well-understood, and easily assessed. Often, in order to provide a suitable descriptive comment for a reproduction, it is enough to name the object represented, and the rest is a matter of course.

If interpretations were as well understood as reproductions, a descriptive comment of the form: "this is an interpretation of that" would generally do. But we are far from from this. All representations which are neither plain descriptions, nor plain reproductions are commonly referred

12

to as *interpretation*. There is no obvious reason to assume that all these have much in common and constitute a distinct kind of representation, rather than a vast and vague residual category.

Two types of definition have been put forward: interpretations have been characterized either as representations based on subjective under-standing, or as representations faithful to the meaning rather than to the directly observable aspects of the things represented. By diluting the notion of meaning to the point of irrelevance, both definitions can actu-ally be made to coincide. But how are we to characterize interpretations, at least ethnographic ones, without resorting to such a ploy?

Representations commonly called "interpretations" do indeed seem to involve a compromise between objectivity and more subjective considera-tions: the desire to be understood, to put matters in a certain light, a compromise between adequacy to the things represented and effective-ness in forming and conveying ideas. Does this relative subjectivity, this character of a compromise define a homogeneous category of representa-tions? It could be argued, rather, that any representation involves a con-cern for both empirical adequacy and pragmatic effectiveness. In plain cases of description, or of reproduction, the constraints imposed by the search for truth, or for resemblance, are so strong as to be the only ones noticed. In most cases of so-called "interpretation," the search for em-pirical adequacy seems less constraining; the compromise between it and the intent of the interpreter is more apparent. Actually, when a descrip-tion is openly speculative, or when a reproduction involves intentional distortions, they too are called "interpretations." Interpretation so under-stood is at best an heterogeneous category. It is not characterized by a specific mode of empirical adequacy, nor does it call for a particular type of descriptive comment. In this loose sense, with which we shall not be concerned anymore, all sciences, of course, and not just the social sci-ences, are interpretive, since they are forever speculative.

Defining interpretations much more narrowly as representations faith-ful to the meaning of the thing interpreted only makes sense in specific cases, translations or summaries for instance. What is interpreted in these cases is a text, i.e., an object for which the notion of meaning is relatively clear (clear, at least, when compared to the notion of meaning as applied to a ritual or to a work of art). The linguistic notion of meaning is closely linked to that of sameness of meaning. Sameness of meaning makes it possible for one text – the interpretation – to represent the meaning of another text.

This semantic characterization of interpretations is clearly too narrow to account for their role in the social sciences. Interpretations, here, are not only of texts. In ethnography for instance, all aspects of human thought and behavior are interpreted. Even interpretations of verbal ma-

13

terials, of myths for example, aim far beyond a mere representation of their textual meaning.

What are, then, ethnographic interpretations? What kind of knowledge do they bear? Could they be given adequate descriptive comments and be used as scientific evidence? Lacking *a priori* answers, we should perhaps look at the way ethnographers actually go about interpreting. Here, I shall consider but a single example: the combination of an anecdote, a gloss, and a generalization borrowed from the justly famous study of Nuer religion by Evans-Pritchard (1956). The problems I shall discuss are by no means specific to this work. Take any book of ethnography and you are almost sure to find several similar examples.

True, in some works of ethnography, little space is given to the interpretation of cultural phenomena. An ethnographer may, for instance, study the economy or the demography of a society on the basis of a statistical exploitation of descriptive data. However, to the extent that this work is truly ethnographic, i.e., considers the economy or the demography in its relationship to the culture, interpretations of cultural phenomena, whether long or short, play a crucial role. All ethnographic (or for that matter historical) interpretations face the same epistemological problems. It is these problems, rather than ethnography in general, that will be discussed here.

Interpretations in ethnography

At their most factual level, ethnographic accounts seem typically to consist of a mixture of descriptions and quotations. Take for instance the following anecdote told by Evans-Pritchard:

The anecdote

I was present when a Nuer was defending himself against silent disapproval on the part of his family and kinsmen of his frequent sacrifices. He had been given to understand that it was felt that he was destroying the herd from inordinate love of meat. He said that this was not true. . . . It was all very well for his family to say that he had destroyed the herd, but he had killed the cattle for their sakes. It was "*kokene yiekien ke yang*," "the ransom of their lives with cattle." He repeated this phrase many times as one by one he recounted cases of serious sickness in his family and described the ox he had sacrificed on each occasion to placate the spirit *deng* (Evans-Pritchard 1956: 222).

This is about as raw a factual account as you will ever find in most ethnographic works. Yet not a single statement in it expresses a plain observation.

"Silent disapproval" cannot be observed but only surmised. Similarly, that a man "had been given to understand that it was felt that . . ." is an inference from a variety of often ambivalent and complex behaviors. These inferences are likely to have been made not directly by the ethnog-

14

rapher, but by his informants. The resulting description is actually what the ethnographer selected from what he understood of what his informants told him of what they understood.

The rest of the account is not so much description as quotation. More accurately, it is a report in indirect style (with the exception of one directly quoted formula) of the content, the gist, of a speech as understood, summarized, and translated by the ethnographer with, probably, the help of informants.

Evans-Pritchard put forward this anecdote in order to illustrate the way in which Nuer think of sacrifices and more specifically of those they call *kuk kwoth*. He had already devoted several chapters to Nuer uses of "*kwoth*," a word which he chose to render sometimes by "Spirit" and sometimes by "God." The word "*kuk*" (of which "*kok*" is a verbal form) remained to be explained:

The gloss
The present range of meaning of the word includes buying and selling. . . . Nuer idea of a purchase is that you give something to a merchant who is thereby put under an obligation to help you. At the same time you ask him for something you need from his shop and he ought to give it to you because by taking your gift, he has entered into a reciprocal relationship with you. Hence *kok* has the sense of either "to buy" or "to sell." . . . The general notion conveyed by the word is therefore that of exchange. This sense covers, as do our own words "ransom" and "redemption" both religious and commercial usages (Ibid.: 223-224).

This gloss of *kuk* is quite intuitive. Still, if we do not mistrust the ethnographer's intuitions we too get some intuitive grasp of the meaning of the term. We might find unfelicitous his choice of "ransom" or "redemption" to render *kuk*. This would not matter much as long as, in translations of Nuer statements, we associate "ransom" not with the ordinary English meaning but rather with what we grasped of the meaning of *kuk*.

Such anecdotes and glosses do not suffice to answer the question: how do Nuer think of sacrifice? They are suggestive, though. They foster speculations. Here are Evans-Pritchard's:

The generalization
A *kuk kwoth*, sacrifice to God (or to some spirit), appears to be regarded as a ransom which redeems the person who pays it from a misfortune that would, or might, otherwise fall on him. By accepting the gift, God enters into a covenant to protect the giver of it or help him in some other way. Through the sacrifice man makes a kind of bargain with his God (Ibid.: 221).

It should be apparent that the generalization is only loosely related to the anecdote and the gloss. This looseness partly comes from the fact that the generalization is itself too vague to be open to strong confirmation or disconfirmation.

15

To say that a "sacrifice to God . . . appears to be regarded as a ransom . . ." is about as hedged a statement as possible. Who, actually, "appears to regard?" All Nuer? Most of them? Some of them? When? In general? On some occasions only? In which ways do they "appear" to regard? "Regard," well yes, but how? As a matter of fact? As a favored assumption?

The two other sentences: "God enters into a covenant . . ." and ". . . man makes a kind of bargain . . ." look like more straightforward assertions. The question, however, arises: whose assertions are they? The ethnographer's? That would be most odd: ethnographers do not generally believe in the religions they study. Evans-Pritchard for instance did not believe that God entered into a covenant or was being bargained with in the way described. Is then the ethnographer quoting assertions made by the Nuer? Presumably not, or he would have said so. These statements, though put forward by the ethnographer, are asserted neither by him nor by the Nuer. What they purport to convey is, it seems, a compromise between Nuer thought and the ethnographer's means of expression. In other words, they are typical interpretations.

Such interpretations are extensively used in ethnography along with descriptions and quotations. As illustrated by the anecdote, the gloss, and the generalization cited, most descriptions and quotations are irretrievably interlaced with interpretations, while many more general statements are purely interpretive.

Interpretations help ethnographers convey their understanding of a culture: this is enough to justify their use. This justification is easy to confirm. A simple argument for it is that interpretive accounts are open to assessment: some are more adequate than others, which would not be case if they were all without empirical import.[3] Moreover, it is dubious that what is achieved through interpretation could be achieved by other means. A strictly descriptive approach to facts such as those reported above would be cumbersome if not impracticable; it would discourage readers rather than help them; what purpose would it serve, anyway?

The use of interpretation in ethnography is well warranted. The use of ethnographic interpretations as anthropological evidence is another matter. A necessary condition for such a use is that these interpretations be given adequate descriptive comments. But what should the descriptive comment of an interpretation consist of?

Ethnographic interpretations as "indirect speech"

Ethnographers provide some descriptive comments, however insufficient, for a number of their interpretations. These comments take the standard form of a clause (e.g., "according to the shamans . . .", "The Nuer think that. . .") to which the interpretation proper is apposed or subordinated. By considering these descriptive comments one can form an idea of the range, the variety, and the explicitness of ethnographic interpretations.

The clearest cases are plain translations. Their descriptive comments are similar to those of quotations (e.g., "the man said: '. . .' "), and they can likewise be used as representations of utterances, but only as regards their content.

Many other interpretations are manifestly expressed in the linguistic form known as "indirect speech." In elementary textbook examples, indirect speech differs from direct quotation only in that it occurs in a subordinate clause and involves transposition of pronouns, some adverbs, and tenses. For instance:

He said that he had killed the cattle for their sake

is supposed to be an indirect version of:

He said: "I have killed the cattle for your sake"

If that were really the case, indirect speech would be but a stylistic variant of direct quotation and could be used accordingly. But, in fact, indirect speech can depart from such simple and explicit transposition in at least two ways, and this makes it impossible to recover, even approximately, an initial utterance from an indirect report of it:

a) Indirect speech can be a summary rather than a paraphrase. Thus, "He said that he had killed the cattle for their sake" might summarize a long speech in which the sentence "I have killed the cattle for your sake" need not appear at all.

b) Indirect speech may include elements which were absent from the original and which express the understanding or judgment of the reporter rather than those of the original speaker. For instance, the utterance "I have killed the cattle for your sake" could be reported as:

I heard a man say that the reason why he performed sacrifices was to dispose *kwoth* in favor of his relatives.

There is no way to tell how close an indirect speech report is to some original utterance, how much it condenses, how much it expands. Unlike quotation in the original tongue, and to a much greater extent than translation, indirect speech (ethnographers' favorite style) can lead to quite different reports of the same discourse. In this respect, indirect speech reports are like descriptions: one and the same object can be described in quite different ways. As long as indirect speech reports are about specific speech events, they can be provided with descriptive comments which give them an empirical import comparable to that of descriptions. Nothing in their nature bars such reports from getting confirmed or disconfirmed (even though, in most ethnographic cases, contingent reasons force us to take them on trust), or from being used to confirm or disconfirm other representations.

Problems arise from the fact that "indirect speech" is used to report a much wider and vaguer range of phenomena than just specific speech events. It is used for unattributed speech: "it is said that . . . ," attributed or unattributed thought: "she thought that . . . ," "it was considered that . . . ," and many even less clearly defined objects: "they seem to imply that . . . ," "I understood that . . . ," "it seems to them that . . . ," "he meant that . . . ," etc. In all such cases, there is no question of a transposition or of a summary of a once accessible original: one is dealing with the synthetic fixation of fuzzy sets of sundry data.

Moreover, indirect speech can be left entirely without descriptive comment and presented in a main clause (i.e., without being subordinated to a clause such as "he said that . . .") as for instance in:

It was all very well for his family to say that he had destroyed the herd, but he had killed the cattle for their sake.

This sentence as a whole is indirectly reported speech, but this has to be inferred from contextual and stylistic clues. Still, in this instance of what is known as "free indirect speech," the clues are clear enough to determine an adequate descriptive comment.

In many other cases, it also seems sensible to understand sentences as instances of "free indirect speech," but clues are less clear. Consider again:

Through the sacrifice man makes a kind of bargain with his God.

As was pointed out, this statement could hardly be asserted by the ethnographer, or quoted from something a Nuer said. It is best understood as implicitly subordinate to a main clause like "Nuer appear to think that . . . ," but even such a vague descriptive comment is hazardous.

In literary uses of free indirect speech, a certain degree of indeterminacy as to whether the author or the narrator is making his own point or interpreting someone else's may be intended or at least accepted. Readers are free to understand the text in the manner most relevant to them. Thus what is lost in explicitness is gained in ease of communication. The same type of gain is achieved in ethnography through the use of interpretations without descriptive comment.

Anthropologists, however, do not see their interpretations as the applications of some literary device, but as the outcome of a method or of an epistemological attitude essential to social sciences. They are not aware of using free indirect speech, with all it leaves implicit or vague. If some vagueness remains, they see it as pertaining to the very nature of interpretation, and it behooves philosophers rather than anthropologists to clarify it. Quite a few philosophers have reinforced anthropologists in this view.

Most novelists use free indirect speech the way Molière's Monsieur Jourdain used prose: without knowing that they do so. Actually, a hundred years ago, free indirect speech had not yet been identified by grammarians. Only now is its importance in literature, and in discourse in general, beginning to be recognized.[4] Free indirect speech is the style which allows the author to tell a story "from the point of view of the actors," and the reader to identify with them. The less an identification is conscious, the better it is accepted. There would be nothing surprising or shameful, therefore, if ethnographers too had made extensive use of free indirect speech without being aware of it.

There is, however, one argument which seems to go against reducing the interpretation of cultural phenomena to a specific use of indirect and free indirect speech. Indirect styles are used to report conceptual representations. Conceptual representations come in two forms: ideas, which are private and mental, and messages, which are public and behavioral. The phrase "reported *speech*" is therefore misleading: indirect speech reports can be about any type of conceptual representation whether or not it constitutes the meaning of some verbal message ("utterance," "text," or "discourse"). The category of conceptual representations, although wider than that of meanings, still seems too narrow to encompass all the objects of ethnographic interpretation (and, of course, having taken exception to an *ad hoc* widening of the notion of meaning, we cannot resort to an *ad hoc* widening of the notion of a conceptual representation). Most ethnographic interpretations are, according to their authors, not about conceptual representations, but about institutions. The idea of institutions reported in the free indirect style is even more mysterious than that of interpretation itself; it could not very well serve, therefore, to clarify it.

However, when ethnographers state what their interpretations are about, they may be mistaken. The use of free indirect speech typically causes such mistakes to happen. Say a novelist writes:

Peter walked to the window. It was raining now.

The second sentence seems to be the description of the weather at the time when Peter walked to the window. But, actually, it is a report in the free indirect style, not of what Peter could see, but of the representation he formed of it. Just imagine the passage to be a description of Peter hallucinating: it would be clear, then, that "it was raining now" does not state that it was raining. In ordinary circumstances, however, if Peter thinks he sees that it is raining, then it *is* raining, and readers have no reason to pay attention to the logical difference involved. They may be tempted, rather, to consider that they are given the world to see, but to see "from the Peter's point of view." The literary – or ethnographic – usefulness of such a confusion is obvious, but, logically, a confusion it is.

When one would like to "see things from someone else's point of view," it is, actually, someone else's *representation of things* that one tries to represent to oneself. To be able to infer what things are from a knowledge of the representation Peter has of them, one needs supplementary assumptions: for instance the assumption that Peter sees things the way they are. To believe that one sees things from the point of view of someone else is, thus, to mistake the representation of an object for the object itself, a premise (by itself inconclusive) for the conclusion. Anthropological interpretations characteristically suffer from such a confusion.

What are ethnographic interpretations about?

Ethnographic interpretations seem to fall into two large classes. On the one hand, there are translations and indirect, or free indirect reports of specific speech events, which have, or can easily be given an adequate descriptive comment, and which, therefore, raise no special epistemological issue. On the other hand, there are interpretations of behaviors or institutions such as sacrifice, marriage, initiation, war, divination, potlatch, table manners, etc. The epistemological relationship between interpretations of this second class and their objects seems mysterious, a descriptive comment seems impossible.

On closer examination, however, there is no mystery, only a confusion. The epistemological haziness is not due to an impalpable halo surrounding interpretive understanding, but to an error of focus. The true object of any interpretation is a conceptual representation (or a set of representations which it synthesizes). The representation interpreted has itself an object. The error consists in focusing on the object of the representation interpreted rather than on that representation itself.

With interpretations of the first class, there is little risk of an error. When the ethnographer translates *kokene yiekien ke yang* by "the ransom of their lives with cattle," when he reports in the free indirect style "he had killed the cattle for their sake," he acts as the interpreter of utterances he himself heard. These utterances were about a Nuer sacrifice; the ethnographer's interpretations, however, are about the utterances and not about the sacrifice; here a mistake is unlikely.

On the other hand, with interpretations of the second class, mistakes have to be forestalled, or else they are bound to occur. The object, this time, is not a specific verbal representation, but a set of scattered representations which the interpretation synthesizes. The representations interpreted may well have but one thing in common: their object. The synthesis did not emerge from the whole set of representations considered simultaneously.It developed progressively in the mind of the ethnographer from partial syntheses revised in the light of new data and assumptions. The descriptive comment is succinct (e.g., "For the Nuer, . . .") or altogether lacking. The set of representations interpreted is, at this stage, too fuzzy to be apprehended at all. The object common to all these representations, on the other hand, neatly stands out. It is hard, then, not to mistake the object of the representations interpreted for the object of the interpretation.

When, for instance, Evans-Pritchard writes: "Through the sacrifice man makes a kind of bargain with his God," he synthesizes quite diverse data: conventional formulae, occasional utterances, informants' answers, presuppositions or implicit contents he thought he perceived, hypotheses, impressions, partial syntheses, etc. All these data are conceptual representations, whether verbal, or purely mental. The ethnographer brought them together because he saw them as as being all about the same thing, namely sacrifice. His interpretation of these representations is the most relevant information he can give on Nuer sacrifice, and that is his reason for putting it forward. From there to naming that interpretation an interpretation of Nuer sacrifice, there is but a short step. Yet, from an epistemological point of view, it is a step over the edge.

Why not say, one might query, that an interpretation has *two* objects: a set of mediatory representations, which is the primary object, and the object of these representations themselves, which is the secondary (and often the most important) object of the interpretation?[5] Because it would be impossible, then, to characterize interpretations in terms of a consistent criterion of empirical adequacy: except in those cases where the primary object would happen to be an adequate representation of the secondary object, all interpretations would be inadequate to at least one of their objects. For example, an adequate interpretation of the Book of Genesis is not an adequate description of the beginnings of the Universe, and conversely. An interpretation does not represent its hypothetical secondary object – which is only an apparent object – it represents a representation of it.

It would be unreasonable, however, to hope to change our linguistic usage and to request that, instead of "interpretation of sacrifice," one would say "interpretation of representations of sacrifice." But let it be remembered, then, that this usage is equivocal. The complement of the noun "interpretation," or the direct object of the verb "to interpret" may refer either to what the interpretation is about, or to what the representations interpreted are about.

Notwithstanding linguistic usage, all interpretations in the cultural sciences are representations of conceptual representations. An interpretation is adequate to its object when it is faithful to it, that is when it shares its relevant conceptual properties. For instance, an adequate translation has, as much as possible, the same content as the text translated, an adequate summary expresses the same main ideas as the representation it summarizes, etc. There are only apparent objections, then, to considering that the linguistic forms of anthropological interpretation are those of reported speech, ranging from the direct style of translation to the free indirect style of general interpretations.

Peering through the haze caused by systematic use of free indirect speech, synthetic interpretations of unspecified data, and a complacent epistemology, one should see that cultural ethnography, whatever its apparent objects, is essentially about representations. No great mystery there. An ethnographer does not just observe say sacrifices. She asks about sacrifices, she hears people talk about them. even when she witnesses a few sacrifices, it takes what she has heard to make sense of what she sees. She also broods over what she has seen and heard, tries to imagine what it may be like to perform a sacrifice, what frame of mind it may require, what mood it may evoke. She tries to match what she thinks people think with what she thinks she would think if she were one of them. The work of ethnographers consists both in collecting and in producing representations. Interpreting these representations, that is reporting them as faithfully as possible in the indirect style, is a straightforward way of conveying what they have learnt.

All these representations could conceivably play a mediatory role and help us get to know sacrifice in itself (inasmuch as sacrifice does exist in itself, which is open to question). For this to be the case, one should have some understanding of how these representations represent sacrifice and how ethnographic interpretations represent these representations. In this respect, most ethnographic interpretations – whatever their other merits – are hopelessly vague.

Ethnographers maintain a fiction according to which all the representations synthesized in their interpretations are genuine and truthful descriptions kindly provided by the people whom they call, off-handedly and rather naively, "informants."[6] Actually, the ethnographer's own intuitive representations play a frequent and irreplaceable role. Furthermore, even when the representations interpreted are genuine native expressions, it does not follow that they are descriptions: natives too can quote or interpret. For instance, was the intention of the Nuer quoted by Evans-Pritchard, when repeating "*kokene yiekien ke yang,*" to inform his audience (his relatives and the ethnographer) that in his opinion sacrifice was a kind of ransom, and that he had paid such ransom, etc., or was he himself

22

quoting a traditional formula in order to force his critics either to challenge tradition, or to let him be? Many statements of this kind are never *made* but always *quoted* – and that may be precisely what makes them "cultural." As long as no attention is given to sorting the ethnographer's intuitive understanding from native statements and, among the latter, those made from those quoted, ethnographic interpretations cannot be given an adequate descriptive comment.

As they are, ethnographic interpretations help readers get some understanding of what it is like to share in a different culture. Most ethnographers, however, have further ambitions. They want their work to serve as a basis for anthropological or philosophical generalizations. Ethnography is surrounded by writings of an apparently theoretical character, with their hypotheses and their jargon. What are they really about?

Interpretive terms

Interpretations may involve a peculiar use of terms. Systematic interpretation, as in ethnography, may even lead to the development of an *ad hoc* terminology.

Back to the Nuer case. We saw how the ethnographer expounded his understanding of the word *kuk*, and, for lack of an English equivalent, chose to render it by "ransom," a word, he claimed, with a somewhat comparable import. In translations of Nuer statements, then, "ransom" was to be understood as conveying not its usual meaning but what had been suggested of the meaning of *kuk*. Yet, surely, the ethnographer intended more than just to stipulate a translation convention. He also wanted the standard meaning of "ransom" to remain present in the minds of his readers and to color their understanding of *kuk*. This is blatant when "ransom" is used not in translations but in indirect speech contexts ranging from reports of actual speech events to interpretations of Nuer thought in general. How much exactly of its standard import should the word "ransom" keep or recover in these contexts? This is left for the reader to decide. But at least it is clear that the ethnographer intended the statement:

a *kuk kwoth* appears to be regarded as a ransom

to convey more than just:

a *kuk kwoth* appears to be regarded as a *kuk*.

When a word is thus used in translations and in indirect speech contexts, when it is intended both as a rendering by stipulation of a native category and as a clue for the proper understanding of that category, we are dealing with an interpretive use of a term. When in a text, or in a literary genre such as ethnography, a term is always used interpretively, I shall call it an *interpretive term*.

Even without explicit indication, interpretive terms should be understood as if standing between inverted commas. Their standard meaning does not enter in the global meaning of the sentence in which they occur. That standard meaning at best serves to evoke another meaning, that of the category that the term is used to interpret. Interpretive terms carry no ontological implications: the ethnographer could without contradiction both maintain that Nuer sacrifices are "ransoms paid to God," and deny that God exists or that ransoms of any kind are actually paid.

In this example, "ransom" and "God" are quite explicitly interpretive terms. Most of the terms believed to have a theoretical status in the study of cultural phenomena are also nothing but interpretive terms, even though anthropologists are usually not aware of that fact.

There is a large technical vocabulary in anthropology. Its shortcomings have often been pointed out. Edmund Leach, for instance, has underscored the arbitrary and often ethnocentric character of anthropological terms. Rodney Needham has convincingly argued that most of these terms do not correspond to precise concepts, but rather to "polythetic" notions , that is classes of phenomena having no more in common than a "family resemblance" (to use Wittgenstein's phrase).[7] The reason for this is, I suggest, that anthropological vocabulary developed in response not to theoretical concerns but to interpretive needs.

Many of the native notions ethnographers study also involve a family resemblance between the objects referred to by the same term, rather than a well-understood set of truth-conditions. In other words, two such objects may have little more in common than a resemblance, each in a different respect, to a third object falling under the same term. Such notions are often salient in a culture. "Love" in English is a case to the point: what justifies sensual love and one's love of truth coming under the same term is that both share some features, albeit different ones, with love for someone. If Nuer *kwoth* and *kuk* are problematical, it is because they too, it seems, are family resemblance notions. Such fuzzy notions usually have no synonyms in their own language, let alone in the language of the ethnographer.

Ethnographers also study terms referring to social positions and institutions, which, of course, vary from culture to culture. These terms usually carry a single complex truth-condition, namely, that some competent agency should, formally or informally, explicitly or implicitly, have acknowledged that the term applies. What makes a vizir "vizir," a Pope "Pope," or a guru "guru" is to have been appointed, elected, or chosen as such; what makes a "congress," a "battalion," a "jihad," or a "*kuk kwoth*" is to have been convened, formed, declared, or intended as such by the competent individual or group. As a result of this peculiar type of single truth-condition, these terms have no synonym in their own language and no translation in others (unless, that is, the competent agency decides otherwise, as when the Catholic Church itself provides translations for "Pope").

When a term is without straightforward translation, there are three possibilities: one may approximate its meaning by means of a term having comparable pragmatic implications, which amounts to mistranslating it somewhat (as when Arab *jihad* is rendered by "Holy War"); one may borrow the term rather than translate it (as "vizir" or "guru" in English); or one may render it by a word stripped of its standard meaning and used with a stipulated meaning (as, for instance, when anthropologists use "mother's brother" to refer not only to the mother's actual brothers but also to some of her male cousins). The difference between these three devices is not always clear-cut. Approximations may be recognized as such, and mentally rectified, as if in accordance with a tacit stipulation (a Polynesian leader may be referred to as a "king" without careful readers forming a wrong picture). The original meaning of a borrowed term may be partly lost or altered, hence borrowing does not preclude mistranslation (thus to translate the Hindu "guru" by the now English word "guru" does not guarantee proper understanding). A term used with a stipulated meaning may nevertheless have been chosen because of the near appositeness of its original meaning, the memory of which may then introduce a bias (as, arguably, in Evans-Pritchard's use of the term "ransom," with its inappropriate Christian connotations).

Anthropologists' technical vocabulary is a medley of words to be used where straightforward translations are wanting: "sacrifice," "divination," "priest," "shaman," "totem," "taboo," "symbol," "marriage," "warfare," "king," "feudalism," "caste," "tribe," etc., are approximations generally acknowledged as such, borrowed terms the original meaning of which fades away, terms with a stipulated meaning superimposed on the original one. Yet this technical vocabulary is not only used in translation but also in freer forms of interpretation.

The Nuer have, according to Evans-Pritchard, two words for the ritual slaughter of an animal and a variety of words and phrases for the many rites which seem to culminate in such a slaughter, or in the offering of a cucumber as a substitute. The ethnographer refers to all these, and to them only, as "sacrifices." The rites thus referred to differ widely. They fall neither under a single Nuer named category, nor under a universal definition. They do not always include a slaughter. They share no more than a family resemblance. In this context, then, the meaning of "sacrifice" must be understood either as fundamentally vague, or, more charitably, as a disjunction of the meanings of all the Nuer words and phrases that Evans-Pritchard decided to render by "sacrifice:" "sacrifice" means "the rites that the Nuer call this, or the rites that the Nuer call *kuk kwoth*, or the rites that the Nuer call that, or etc." "Sacrifice" is thus a synthetic interpretive term: it is used to render not one Nuer category, but several.

It might be argued that the ethnographer dwells on Nuer views of "sacrifice" without bothering to establish that they have the concept, and thereby imposes on the Nuer conceptual framework, if not an alien category, at least an alien grouping of categories. Moreover, from a comparative point of view, a notion of sacrifice which applies only to the Nuer without being a Nuer notion may seem altogether unfit.

However sensible, such criticisms of the use of technical terms in anthropology are somewhat beside the point. They would be fatal if they applied to descriptive scholarship. In interpretation many of the shortcomings objected to become assets. Ethnographic interpretation aims at making an alien experience at least intuitively intelligible. The difficulties are, to an important extent, due to differences in conceptual frameworks. To overcome these difficulties, universally defined notions are of no interpretive value, and true borrowings of idiosyncratic native terms take a lot of glossing over and can only go so far. Superimpositions, blurrings, and blendings of meanings, stipulation of *ad hoc* categories are, on the other hand, quite effective devices.

Thus the ethnographer's seemingly odd notion of sacrifice makes it possible to ask a variety of questions and to speculate over Nuer data. Should these questions prove arbitrary, these speculations random, still, going into them will have fostered a moderate sense of familiarity with some Nuer ways, while conveying, one hopes, the problematical character of it all. This limited achievement hinges on the fact that "sacrifice" is used interpretively. Its stipulated meaning recapitulates all and only those Nuer categories which seem close enough to some universal notion of sacrifice. In this context, "sacrifice" is mediatory between Nuer and Western scholarly notions, and hence differs from either of these. An interpretive term is resorted to because it is felt that familiar notions are insufficient either to translate or to describe alien ones.

Interpretive generalizations

One might grant that, in ethnography, technical terms are used interpretively, and yet inquire: is this also the case in theoretical anthropology? Take, for instance, "sacrifice." According to various theories, sacrifice is at the origin, or at the core of religion or even of culture as a whole; it is an act of communion, or of separation, or a gift, or the setting up of a scapegoat; various stages, roles, and functions should be distinguished, etc. How is the object of such theories defined?

Often, an *a priori* definition is offered; for instance: sacrifice is the slaughter of an animal or human as an offering to some supernatural being. This merely looks like a definition. A theory of sacrifice is intended to account equally well for Nuer "sacrifice," Hindu "sacrifice," Greek "sacrifice," Bororo "sacrifice," etc. But, each time, "sacrifice" has a different sense. In each of these cases, sacrifice is an interpretive term which renders more or less adequately an ensemble of native categories. These categories generally encompass complex rites of which a slaughter is only one element: the slaughter may be preceded by invocations, libations, purifications, and followed by culinary preparations, divinatory practices, etc. Sometimes, a single native category, which the ethnographer renders by "sacrifice," covers slaughters, vegetable offerings, and rites which apparently do not involve any kind of offering at all.

Ethnographers, though, do not decide at random to call some rite a "sacrifice." They usually do so because that rite resembles in some way other rites already described in the literature as "sacrifices." These rites, in turn, owe their name to a resemblance to other, previously described rites, and so on. It would be a mistake to look for some initial decision which would be at the origin of the anthropological study of sacrifice; the first anthropological uses of the term themselves imitated Christian reinterpretations of ancient Jewish, Greek, or Roman religious uses.

When anthropologists state: "Sacrifice is the slaughter of an animal or human as an offering to some supernatural being," they are not giving a definition, they are interpreting an idea common to most Western interpretations – whether religious or ethnographic – of sacrificial rites. When they seem to be developing a theory of sacrifice, they are, actually, pursuing this work of second (or *n*th) degree interpretation, though in a more speculative fashion. They take some ethnographic interpretations (or, sometimes, directly appropriate some native representations) and generalize them to all sacrifices. Robertson Smith, for instance, put forward an essentially "Semitic" view of sacrifice; Hubert and Mauss were applying to sacrifice in general a synthesis of Vedic and Biblical ideas; Edmund Leach recently proposed a "Biblical" theory, etc.[8]

For ethnographers, these theories are sources of interpretive inspiration, repertoires of possible "meanings;" they may be adopted, adapted or rejected at will, according to the case under study. Thus, when Evans-Pritchard discusses what he calls the "meaning" of Nuer sacrifice in the light of "theories of sacrifice," he remarks:

The communion theory as held by Robertson Smith . . . gives us little aid towards understanding the nature of Nuer sacrifices to God. (Evans-Pritchard 1956: 274)

What Georges Gusdorf says of religious sacrifice in general, that it is made not only to the gods but against the gods, is very true for the Nuer. (ibid.: 275)

The ideas of purchase, redemption, indemnification, ransom, exchange, bargain, and payment are very evident in Nuer sacrifices . . . they are not peculiar in this, for, as Hubert and Mauss rightly emphasize, there is probably no sacrifice in which there is not some idea of redemption and something of the nature of a contract. (ibid.: 276)

Ethnographers turn to such theories when they can borrow from them some vague formula (sacrifice is made "against the gods," it contains "something of the nature of a contract") in order to interpret their own data. When such theories fall into disuse (as, for instance, the once fashionable astronomical and meteorological interpretations of religious symbols) it is in the manner of tools which have become obsolete. This obsolescence is only in part due to the fact that ethnographers have a better knowledge of a wider range of cases, and are in need of more sophisticated interpretations. Ethnographers and their public belong to a rapidly changing culture: interpretive generalizations which once might have helped convey some intuitive grasp of alien ways may themselves become alien and thereby lose their usefulness. Similarly, new interpretations may be preferred not because they are more adequate to the facts, but because they are, for the time being, better adapted to an ever changing public.

Interpretive generalizations are not, properly speaking, confirmable or disconfirmable theories. They are usable or unusable tools. Could it be otherwise? Could interpretive generalizations constitute genuine theories? To answer that question, one should consider not only the uses, but also the logic of interpretive generalizations, and one should compare it to the logic of descriptive generalizations. Here I shall only put forward a rudimentary sketch of such a comparison.

A descriptive generalization answers the double question: What is empirically possible? What is empirically impossible? For instance, "all elephants are gray" implies that it is possible for an object to be both an elephant and gray, and impossible for an object to be both an elephant and not gray. Each observation of a gray elephant corroborates this generalization, but however high the number of corroborations, a single indisputable observation of a white elephant is enough to jeopardize the generalization. This is what makes it so difficult, and so exciting, to discover new descriptive generalizations which are neither trivial nor easily disconfirmed. Scientific theories consist of such descriptive generalizations.

Interpretive generalizations do not in any way specify what is empirically possible or impossible. They provide a fragmentary answer to a simple single question: what is epistemologically feasible? Not: How are things? But: What representation can be given of things? To say, for instance, that all sacrifices are communions, is merely to state that anything that can be interpreted as a sacrifice can be interpreted as a communion. Such a statement may be easy or hard to corroborate (Evans-Pritchard's interpretations, for instance, did not corroborate it), but it is beyond falsification.

In spite of a superficial parallelism, interpretive generalizations differ radically from descriptive generalizations. An interpretation is adequate when it is faithful, a description is adequate when it is true. Faithfulness can be greater or lesser, whereas there are only two truth values: "true" and "false." A description is false from the moment one of its implications is false (even though, in ordinary language, we may then talk of "partial" or "relative truth"). Therefore, a descriptive generalization, which has a great number, or even an infinity of implications, can be falsified in a great number, or even in an infinity of ways; its empirical import is greater than that of a specific description, and so is its vulnerability. Inversely, the more general an interpretation, the less it has empirical import, and the less it is vulnerable to empirical considerations (it may well be more vulnerable to changes of fashion, however): the words and the thoughts of an individual, a Nuer sacrificer for instance, can be interpreted with great faithfulness (it is not easy, of course, there is no guarantee of success, but the project is not absurd); a synthetic interpretation of the Nuer view of sacrifice cannot be equally faithful to the thought of each Nuer on the matter (unless one assumes that they all think identically, which is hardly plausible); a general interpretation of sacrifice, in every place and time, synthesizes not empirical data, but interpretations which are themselves already synthetic. Such general interpretation bears at best only a distant and occasional relationship to the thought of individuals involved in "sacrifices."

Interpretive generalizations are not the still clumsy expressions of an immature anthropological science, they are the old-fashioned props of ethnography, a now mature discipline which should be able to do without them.

Explaining and interpreting cultural representations

The monogamous and jealous union of ethnography and anthropology, which are taught in the same departments, practiced by the same scholars, with hardly any effort to distinguish two approaches and two aims, has hampered both disciplines. Anthropology receives from ethnography inappropriate concepts and irrelevant issues. An important part of its energy is spent on trying to answer such questions as: What is totemism? Sacred kingship? What is the meaning of sacrifice? What are the respective parts of descent and alliance in kinship? Do all cultures have myths?

A form of science? What is the function of witchcraft? What are the differences between religion and magic? Possession and shamanism? All these questions are ill posed. They are framed in interpretive terms. There is no *a priori* reason to assume that these terms correspond to homogeneous and distinct classes of phenomena, i.e., to potential objects of scientific inquiry. Entangled in these pseudo-concepts and pseudo-questions, anthropologists fail to reach a consensus on the fundamental issues and aims of their discipline, or even on a general characterization of cultural phenomena.

Let us, however, try: humans are naturally able to build, memorize, and communicate mental representations (abilities which, of course, need a proper environment in which to develop, in particular, the company of other human beings). Every day each individual builds thousands of mental representations; most of these are almost immediately forgotten, and are never transmitted. Very few mental representations are expressed, that is, transformed into public representations and thus transmitted to others. The vast majority of transmitted representations are transmitted only once. A few representations, however, are retransmitted by their initial receivers to new receivers who, in turn, retransmit them, and so on. A social network, more or less extended in space and time, is thus penetrated by a representation. We are now dealing with a specifically cultural representation which consists of a multiplicity of mental and public versions related to one another both by their genesis and by the similarity of their contents. The set of all such representations which circulate within a human group constitutes its culture. By extension, any phenomena, be it an event, a tool, a building, a practice, a habit, a food, etc., which is in part determined by these specifically cultural representations can be called cultural too. In particular, in this extended sense, all mental representations, even those which are communicated only once, even those which are never communicated, are to some extent cultural; they are conceived and processed in the context of a partially shared knowledge; they are, in some respects, peripheral versions, idiosyncratic transformations of common representations.

There is one question that any scientific anthropology should answer (whether directly or indirectly): through which process of selection, as a function of what factors, does a tiny fraction of all the mental representations that humans build become shared cultural representations, and invade, either temporarily (rumors, fashions), or lastingly (traditions) the networks of social communication? A cultural anthropology must comprise – I am tempted to say, must be – an epidemiology of ideas.

The idea of an epidemiology of ideas is not entirely new. It is implicit in the debate between evolutionists and diffusionists which agitated anthropology at the turn of the century, as well as in several recent works.[9]

Lévi-Strauss's *Mythologiques* can be seen as an "epidemiology of myths."[10] More recently, two teams of biologists, L.L. Cavalli-Sforza and M.W. Feldman, in a cautious way, and Charles Lumsden and Edward O. Wilson more ambitiously, have proposed models borrowed from population biology, and from epidemiology in particular, to account for the evolution and the diffusion of cultural phenomena.[11] Whatever their other merits, these biologically inspired models are based on a superficial understanding of cultural representations.

Unlike genes, viruses, or bacteria, which normally reproduce, and only exceptionally undergo a mutation, mental representations have a basically unstable structure: the normal fate of an idea is to become altered or to merge with other ideas; what is exceptional is the reproduction of an idea. Hence, as indirectly suggested by the work of Lévi-Strauss, an epidemiology of ideas must deal as much with the transformation of ideas as with their reproduction. To put it differently, the strict reproduction of an idea should be seen as a limiting case: the degree zero of transformation. An epidemiology of ideas will, therefore, need more than customized biological models; it will have to rely heavily on a psychology of mental representations.[12]

Cognitive psychology has undergone considerable development in the past twenty years,[13] but few are the works which deal with the problem of specifically cultural representations.[14] No study, as far as I know, directly attempts to explain, on the basis of cognitive psychological considerations, why some ideas are more contagious than others.[15] On the other hand, there are many works bearing , for instance, on concept formation, memory for narratives, or understanding of metaphors, which are suggestive in this respect.[16]

What can be predicted, in such conditions of the future of anthropology? Pessimists might note that biologists approach the study of cultural phenomena with preconceived and superficial ideas, that psychologists, on their part, neglect this study in spite of the fact that they are better equipped to contribute to it, and, lastly, that anthropologists usually ignore these other disciplines and go in all directions at the same time, that is to say nowhere. Optimists might note, on the contrary, elements of convergence between biology, psychology, and anthropology, they might pay attention (which I cannot do here) to various new trends in anthropology, and they would then predict the rebirth of a truly general anthropology, or even the birth of a scientific anthropology. I do not know who, of the pessimists and the optimists, would be better prophets, but it seems more interesting, and more productive, to bet on the optimists, and to do one's best to make their prediction come true.

It should be possible to confirm or disconfirm truly anthropological hypotheses by using evidence provided by ethnography, among other

31

sources. The interpretive character of most ethnographic data does not, in this respect, constitute a fundamental obstacle: interpretations can serve as scientific evidence provided they come with an appropriate descriptive comment that clarifies their empirical import. It would make no sense, however, for ethnographers to aim at collecting in advance the evidence that a scientific anthropology might one day have a use for.

Ethnographers aim, quite appropriately, at a systematic coverage, both from a geographic and from a thematic point of view, of all the cultural groups which inhabit or have inhabited the earth. Such a coverage is bound to bring together much more information than anthropology could ever use, and to bypass evidence which, at some juncture, might turn out to be of crucial relevance to anthropological theorizing. The truly anthropological work of Berlin and Kay on the classification of colors illustrates the point: Berlin and Kay developed the hypothesis that all color classifications, in spite of the fact that they seem to vary arbitrarily from one language to another, are based on a small number of universal basic color categories. There were, in the literature, plenty of ethnographic reports on color classification, but, having been gathered without theoretical perspective, most of them lacked this or that bit of information which would have been essential to put Berlin and Kay's hypothesis to the test. The publication of their work stimulated the collection of until then neglected data. This new evidence has corroborated their initial assumptions and has made it possible to revise them on minor points.[17]

Ethnographers are often the only ones who can provide the scholarly community with some knowledge of the society in which they worked. As a result, they may have to answer the queries of historians, geographers, economists, linguists, and fellow anthropologists or ethnographers. Actually, ethnographic questionnaires preceded, in the nineteenth century, the professionalization of anthropology, and are still one of its tools. This, however, is only a peripheral aspect of ethnographic work.

All the representations that humans conceive and convey are, as I said, cultural to some degree, in an extended sense of the term. It is the more cultural representations, i.e., the more widely shared ones, that make it possible to communicate the more individual ones. It is, conversely, the lack of a manifestly shared context – of a common culture – that makes it difficult or even impossible to understand what people of other societies say or do. Ethnographers are first and foremost interpreters who try to render those words and acts intelligible. How can they hope to achieve such an aim?

In the field, ethnographers acquire a knowledge which does not answer any preconceived queries, and the relevance of which pertains, on the contrary, to the questions it raises. While observing in others another way of being human, ethnographers come to sense it latent in themselves. In fact, should they fail to discern it in themselves, they would fail to properly perceive it in others. For the main part, the work of ethnographers consists in acquiring, and then conveying that knowledge.

In the field, ethnographers go through a unique experience. Of course, they benefit from the wisdom and the teaching of their predecessors, and from the tools and techniques of the trade, but their main tool is an ensemble of personal relationships by means of which they connect themselves to a cultural network. That tool, ethnographers do not bring in their trunks, they do not even bring a technique to build it: genuine personal relationships are not imposed on others, they are developed jointly, and in accordance with the feelings and ideas of each participant.

The tool is not everything; it requires proper handling. The best ethnographers are not those who have the best personal relationships, but rather, those who best understand these relationships, who recognize what is being transacted, who are capable of interpreting, first for themselves, the representations involved. Here again, no teachable technique replaces the work of intuitive understanding.

Then comes the moment to share this largely intuitive knowledge. Because it is grounded in a unique experience, the problem is each time a new one. Ideally therefore each ethnographer should rethink the ethnographic genre, just as every true novelist rethinks the novel. This is not to say that anybody may without damage do anything, but, on the contrary, that the problem faced by each ethnographer is too specific and too difficult to be tractable in terms of an all-purpose solution, a model to follow, a recipe to apply. Alas, too many ethnographic works, all cast in the mold of the doctoral dissertation, are versions of one another before being dry and distant interpretations of cultural data from which the authors seem to have been longing to extricate themselves.

The relative monotony of ethnographic literature pertains, for a large part, to the convergence of interpretations too much modeled on one another, and too far removed from their object. Of course, ethnographers cannot merely quote and describe. In most cases, they must interpret, that is add to the various native versions that constitute a cultural representation, an atypical, or, which amounts to the same, an exaggeratedly typical, exogeneous version, a distorted version, therefore, but one intelligible and relevant to their readers. Only quotations can be strictly faithful. Any interpretation is a distortion and is unfaithful to some extent. Where quotations are inappropriate, the best interpretation should be, then, the most faithful interpretation compatible with the search for intelligibility and relevance.

For most anthropologists, ethnographic interpretations have another purpose: to give an account of cultural phenomena in a standardized theoretical vocabulary so as to allow for comparisons and theoretical interpretations. I have tried to show that this is an illusory ambition: The technical vocabulary of anthropology is not theoretical but interpretive, and the very idea of an interpretive theory is inconsistent. By standardizing their interpretations, and thus taking them much further than they need to, ethnographers jeopardize the transmission of the knowledge they have acquired in the field, without, for all that, making a better contribution to general knowledge. True, the interpretive monotony of the ethnographic genre helps ethnographers regain their sense of distance vis-à-vis the field, overcome the anxiety it generates, repress the latent otherness they have discovered in themselves. But what kind of an achievement is that? It would be self-deluding, in any case, to mistake this institutionalized form of self-protection for scientific detachment.

The task of anthropology is to explain cultural representations, that is, to describe the mechanisms that cause particular representations to be selected and shared among a social group. The main task of ethnography is to make intelligible the experience of particular human beings as shaped by the social group to which they belong. In order to achieve that aim, ethnographers have to interpret cultural representations shared by these groups. Explaining cultural representations, interpreting them: two autonomous tasks that contribute to our understanding of cultural phenomena. Both can achieve relevance, but in opposite ways: the more general an explanation, the more relevant it is; what makes an interpretation relevant, on the other hand, is not its generality but its depth, that is its faithfulness to the nexus of mental representations that lies under any particular human behavior. Even though they make a lesser use of imagination and a greater one of experience, ethnographers achieve relevance in the manner of novelists: If *War and Peace* is so relevant to us, it not because Tolstoi developed here and there some general remarks, but because the personal experience of a few individuals caught in the upheaval of early nineteenth century Europe contributes, through Tolstoi's interpretation, to the experience of every reader. Similarly, if reading Malinowski's *Argonauts*, Bateson's *Naven*, or Evans-Pritchard's *Nuer Religion* contributes to our understanding of ourselves and of the world in which we live, it is not because of the interpretive generalizations these works contain, it is because they give us an insight into some fragments of human experience, and this, by itself, makes it worth the journey.

2
Apparently irrational beliefs

Extract from my field diary:

Dorze, Southern Ethiopia
Sunday 24 viii 69

Saturday morning old Filate came to see me in a state of great excitement:
"Three times I came to see you, and you weren't there!"
"I was away in Konso."
"I know. I was angry. I was glad. Do you want to do something?"
"What?"
"Keep quiet! If you do it, God will be pleased, the Government will be pleased. So?"
"Well, if it is a good thing and if I can do it, I shall do it."
"I have talked to no one about it: will you kill it?"
"*Kill*? Kill what?"
"Its heart is made of gold, it has one horn on the nape of its neck. It is golden all over. It does not live far, two days' walk at most. If you kill it, you will become a great man!"

And so on . . . It turns out Filate wants me to kill a dragon. He is to come back this afternoon with someone who has seen it, and they will tell me more . . .

Monday 25 viii

Good weather.
The old man with his dragon did not come back. A pity . . .

I had respect and affection for old Filate. He was a very nice, very old man. He was not senile, however, and he was too poor to drink. His excitement on that day was caused by what he had come to tell me, rather than the other way around. All this makes it even more bewildering: how could a sound person believe that there are dragons, not "once upon the time," but there and then, within walking distance? How am I to reconcile my respect for Filate with the knowledge that such a belief is absurd?

This is of course just a concrete instance of a much discussed general problem: how to account for apparently irrational beliefs?[1] One approach consists in claiming that these beliefs are genuinely irrational and the product of some prerational mental processes. I have discussed this old-fashioned view elsewhere (Sperber 1980). Another approach consists in

35

claiming that people of other cultures "live in other worlds," so that what is rational in their world may well appear irrational in ours. This view, known as "cognitive relativism," is supported by many anthropologists and philosophers. It has in part superseded, in part encompassed two other approaches: intellectualism and symbolism. In this chapter, I want to discuss relativism, and to argue for a rationalist alternative.

The chapter has three parts. In the first part, I present, from an anthropological point of view, what I think is the best possible case for relativism.[2] In the second part, I present psychological arguments against relativism. In the third part, I present the rationalist approach I am advocating.

I. ANTHROPOLOGICAL ARGUMENTS

The limits of the intellectualist and the symbolist approaches

It is not very clear what relativists mean when they claim that people of different cultures live in different world. It is clear though that a strong claim is intended. Could the intellectualist or the symbolist approach make such a strong and obscure claim dispensable?

According to the intellectualist approach, apparently irrational beliefs are less irrational than mistaken. they are part of attempted explanations of the world which are developed in a rational way, but on the basis of poor evidence, inadequate patterns of argumentation, lack of awareness of alternatives, etc.

In many societies, the earth is held to be flat: it is easy to see how this belief could be mistaken rather than irrational. And there are plenty of cases, including modern Western ones, for which a similar explanation is straightforward. Robin Horton (1967), by drawing attention to the existence of apparent paradoxes in Western science, has shown how less obvious cases could be described in intellectualist terms. For instance:

There are striking resemblances between psycho-analytic ideas about the individual mind as a congeries of warring entities, and West African ideas about the body as a meeting place of multiples souls (Horton 1967: 139; see also Horton 1961).

In other cases, however, an intellectualist interpretation would seem much overextended. To take but one example, the Fataleka of the Solomon Islands studied by Remo Guidieri maintain not only that the earth is flat, but also that it is the fifth of nine parallel strata among which various entities are distributed: a person's reflection is in stratum three, flutes are in stratum four, crocodiles are in stratum seven, stratum eight is empty, and so on. Could this be a *mistake*? The anthropologist moreover reports:

Apparently irrational beliefs

In all the comments I could gather, the nine strata of the universe are described without the relationship between them and between the entities that inhabit them being made explicit (Guidieri 1980: 47).

It seems that, rather than explaining the world, this stratigraphy itself begs – in vain – for an explanation. Similarly, the world is hard enough to explain without golden-hearted single-horned dragons. It is unclear how, by adding them to the scene, the Dorze would have made the task easier.

So instead of showing how Filate's beliefs turn out to be rational, all the intellectualist has to offer is the meager comfort of a *petitio principii*: if we had all the data . . .

According to the symbolist approach, myths and rituals are irrational only when taken at a superficial literal level. They should be viewed as an indirect expression of cosmological observations, or metaphysical concerns, or classificatory schemas, or moral values, or social relationships (here authors differ).

Clearly, if an indirect, rationally acceptable meaning is the one intended, then the problem raised by literally absurd beliefs are no greater than those raised by literally absurd metaphors. In both cases, the absurdity could be accounted for as a means to signal that a non-literal interpretation is intended. The use of such indirect forms of expression should not throw suspicion on the user's rationality.

The pertinence of the symbolist approach is nicely illustrated by the well-known statement of the Bororo of Central Brazil: "we are red macaws." Reported by Von den Steinen in 1894, it became a favorite example of the primitive's departure from Western commonsense rationality.[3]

It is a good thing, then, that Christopher Crocker was able to reinvestigate the matter in the field. It turns out that (1) only men say "we are red macaws;" (2) red macaws are owned as pets by Bororo women; (3) because of matrilineal descent and uxorilocal residence, men are in important ways dependent on women; (4) both men and macaws are thought to reach beyond the women's sphere through their contacts with spirits.

In metaphorically identifying themselves with red macaws, then, the Bororo . . . seek . . . to express the irony of their masculine condition (Crocker 1977: 192).

So, the enigmatic subject-matter of so many learned discussions turns out to be but an indirect form of expression well within the bounds of commonsense rationality. No doubt, many other puzzling cases around the world could be handled in similar fashion.

Crocker's argument, however, cuts both ways and illustrates also the limits of the symbolist approach. In the course of establishing that "we are red macaws" is a metaphor, he shows how it differs from superficially similar, literally absurd Bororo statements which are not meant figuratively. The "red macaws" metaphor is itself based on a belief in real contacts with spirits.

Apparently irrational beliefs which believers insist are literally true are found everywhere. Symbolist analyses attribute hidden meanings to these beliefs. Yet, when these meanings are, for all we know, hidden from the believers themselves, the suspicion of irrationality remains.

I am afraid no hidden meaning was intended in Filate's request. What he was asking me to do was to kill a dragon, not to decipher a cryptic message.

Relativism at its scientific best

Even after the intellectualist and the symbolist approaches have been applied wherever they seem to work, a large number of cases remains unaccounted for. The attraction of relativism, on the other hand, is that it seems to solve (or dissolve) the problem in each and every case.

Not all version of relativism are worth discussing. One version claims that all beliefs are not only rational but also valid in their cultural context. This type of relativism gives itself the stamp of validity in its own cultural context and forsakes any claim to universal validity. Mary Douglas, for instance, argues for "a theory of knowledge in which the mind is admitted to be actively creating its universe" (Douglas 1975: xviii) in the following terms:

The present concern is focussed on subjective truth . . . This is a generation deeply interested in the liberation of consciousness from control . . . It is part of our culture to recognize at last our cognitive precariousness (Ibid.: xvii, xviii).

In other words relativism is good for us. She then admits, or rather boasts, that her approach "eschews a solid anchorage" (Ibid.: xix).

Relativism can also be formulated so as to be of interest to one who belong to the scientific rather than to the hermeneutico-psychedelic subculture and who is concerned with objective knowledge and well-grounded theories. The formulation I shall propose makes, I think, the best possible sense of relativism. It is not, however, a generally accepted formulation. On the contrary, its implications are likely to put off most relativists. But then, I would argue, the onus is on them to show how a scientifically oriented relativist could avoid these implications.

The relativist slogan, that people of different cultures live in different worlds, would be nonsense if understood as literally referring to physical worlds. If understood as referring to cognized worlds, it would overstate a very trivial point. Of course, worlds as cognized by people of different cultures differ. They even differ in the same person from one moment to the next.

If, however, the worlds referred to are *cognizable worlds*, then the

38

claim need be neither empty nor absurd. Beings with qualitatively different cognitive abilities do live in different worlds in this sense. Such is the case of animal species with different sensory abilities.

Even when sensory abilities are similar, the capacity to synthesize sensory inputs and to abstract from them may still vary. Two species may be affected by the same range of stimuli but select different sets of features on the basis of which to build their inner representations. They might perceive and pay attention to the same features and still organize them in radically different ways. Contrast, for instance, our usual notion of a thing, which is based on visible spatio-temporal continuity, with that of hypothetical species for which basic things would be smells having as peripheral properties light and sound patterns. Even if this hypothetical species shared our environment, and had a sensory equipment similar to ours, it would definitely live in a cognizable world different from ours.

Do cross-cultural differences in cognitive abilities determine, as do cross-species ones, different cognizable worlds? This is an empirical question with no obvious answer – in any case the same answer is not obvious to everyone.

Most anthropologists take for granted that human cognitive abilities are culturally determined. To a limited extent this is uncontroversial: pastoralists acquire an inordinate ability to perceive features of their cattle, together with a large specialized vocabulary. People with telescopes may know of many more celestial bodies. Writing provides an unbounded external memory, and so on. By developing specific tools and skills, cultural groups extend the cognizable world of their members in different directions. These extensions, however important and interesting (see Goody 1977), are no evidence for relativism. They do not explain apparently irrational beliefs. Filate's dragon, for instance, could not very well be claimed to result from his possessing – or lacking – some culture-specific cognitive skill.

To be of relevance, relativism must maintain that fundamental concepts, meanings and, possibly, postulates used in human cognition are culturally determined.[4] Thus the development and differentiation of cognitive abilities, achieved in other species through genetic evolution, would be, in humans, taken over and pushed much further by cultural transmission.

From a relativist point of view, then, all conceptualized information is cultural. What we think of as the sky, birds, eyes, tears, hunger, death, comes in other cultures under concepts which differ from our own, and is therefore perceived differently.

Propositions that can be entertained, expressed, asserted are, according to relativists, language- and culture-specific. Hence it would be unreasonable to expect translations to preserve propositional content across languages. The aim of translation should be more modest:

One general scheme of translation is better than another to the extent that it is simpler, preserves disposition to accept sentences under analysis [i.e. propositions] in response to observation, and preserves similarity in usage (Harman 1973: 107-108).

On this view, when alien beliefs appear irrational, difficulties of translation are generally to blame: in their original formulation, these beliefs were acceptable to rational beings. The translation has failed to preserve this acceptability. It is not surprising, in particular, that the more theoretical assumptions of another culture (e.g., the existence of a witchcraft substance or of spirit possession) should quite often seem irrational: such assumptions relate to actual observations through implicit inferential steps which it is easy for members of the culture, and generally impossible for aliens, to reconstruct. Without this background, no translation can preserve the acceptability of these theoretical assumptions, hence no good translation is possible.

Furthermore, it can be argued that the acceptability of propositions does not rest on observations and inference alone, but also on a number of general *a priori* beliefs, or postulates. Such postulates determine a "world-view" within which the rationality of beliefs is to be assessed. If these postulates are culture-specific, as a strong relativist would claim, it is unclear how they might be translated at all (see Skorupski 1978).

Within such a relativist framework, the fact that some beliefs held in another culture seem irrational is no evidence that they are. It is evidence rather of how poor our understanding of that culture is. The general problem raised by apparently irrational beliefs dissolves in so many ethnographic issues.

Thus we find beliefs in dragons irrational because we take for granted that things such as a heart of gold cannot occur in nature. This could be a cultural postulate of our own. If so Filate may have been too trusting, but not irrationally credulous, in accepting a report that a dragon had been spotted.

Relativism so understood is doubly attractive to ethnographers. First, it gives them some guidance in interpreting their data: beliefs must be interpreted in the context of world-views, and world-views must be reconstructed so as to dispel the appearance of irrationality of particular beliefs. Second, relativism makes ethnographic data relevant to general anthropological issues: Each well-interpreted belief is a piece of evidence as to the degree and manner in which human cognition is culturally determined. Moreover, while relativism displaces intellectualism and symbolism as *solutions* to the problem of apparently irrational beliefs, it provides a framework where the intellectualist and symbolist *models* have an increased applicability: Each cultural world has its own criteria of rational explanation, and its own range of possible metaphors; there are no universal constraints on either.

Why not just adopt relativism and live happily ever after?

II. PSYCHOLOGICAL ARGUMENTS

The cost of relativism

Some of the implications of relativism are unwelcome. To begin with, a relativist in earnest should be either quite pessimistic about the possibility of doing ethnography at all, or extraordinarily optimistic about the abilities of ethnographers.

It is common place that we cannot intuit what, say, cats think. It takes the subtlest handling of rich ethological observations to arrive at simple well-grounded hypotheses in the matter. If members of other cultures live in different cognizable world, one thing we can take for granted is that these worlds are much more complex than that of cats. How, then, can we get to know them? Shouldn't we conclude, with Rodney Needham, that "the solitary comprehensible fact about human experience is that it is incomprehensible" (Needham 1972: 246)?

Ethnographers feel, however, that, after some months of fieldwork, they are in a position to provide a reasonable if incomplete account of an alien culture. Most of them modestly refrain from explaining this feat. Others attribute it to some mysterious human capacity of comprehension – or better-sounding *Verstehen* – which somehow transcends the boundaries of cognizable worlds. Philosophers in the hermeneutic tradition have extensively discussed this alleged capacity. Ultimately it would fall to psychologists to describe and explain it. At present explaining comprehension *within* a single cognizable world seems great enough a task.

Relativism should cause a more immediate and even greater problem for developmental psychology.[5] Cognitive development (whether of the mind as a whole, or of each distinct cognitive ability) can be viewed as a series of states from an initial one at birth to a mature state. The task of developmental psychology is to describe and explain the passage from one state to another, and, globally, from the initial to the mature state. Relativism implies that the distance between the initial and the mature state is much greater than is usually assumed: it implies that the first stage of cognitive development consists not in acquiring knowledge in an essentially predetermined cognizable world, but, rather, in establishing in which world knowledge is to be acquired. Of course, the greater the distance between the initial and the mature state, the heavier the task of the developing organism, and of psychology.

On the whole, relativists show little concern for, or even awareness of the psychological implications of their views. Worse, they tend to misconceive them. Arguments and evidence in favor of relativism are generally thought to lend support to an anti-innatist view of the human mind. But, I shall argue, this is quite mistaken.

In explaining how the mind develops from state n into state $n+1$, the psychologist can invoke two classes of factors: internal and environmental. Internal factors comprise all the cognitive abilities that the mind possesses in state n. Environmental factors comprise all the input information which is accessible to the mind while in state n and which contributes (in little understood ways) to its moving to state $n+1$. In the initial state at least, the internal factors are essentially innate.

What little understanding we have at present of internal factors is almost entirely speculative. Environmental factors, on the other hand, are open to observation and experimentation. We have some rough idea of what input is accessible to the child at various stages. One generally accepted point about this input is that it is more chaotic than the knowledge developed on the basis of it. This well-known discrepancy between experience and knowledge is the main source of evidence for speculation about internal factors.

Now, relativists are bound to consider that the information accessible in the initial stage of cognitive development is even more chaotic than a non-relativist would hold , since it is not bound by the constraints of a predetermined cognizable world. If one wants to pursue this seriously, one must then assume that the initial state is rich enough to exploit this hyper-chaotic initial input in order to develop the structure of the appropriate cognizable world.

Imagine an organism capable of developing the cognitive abilities of either the cat or the dog, depending, say, on whether it was raised among cats or among dogs. For this, it would need to possess innate abilities sufficient to match those of either species, plus some extra device capable of determining in which of the two cognizable worlds it had landed. It takes richer innate capacities to learn to be a cat or to be a dog than to be either. In the case of humans (as seen by relativists) the surplus of innate capacities required in order to determine the right cognizable world would be incommensurably greater since there are not two, but an infinity of profoundly different accessible worlds, each of a great complexity.

Or take the case of linguistic relativism, which is somewhat better understood than that of cultural relativism. It is clear that humans are capable of acquiring any one of a great variety of languages. This raises the three following questions:

1. How diverse are human languages?
2. How complex are the innate abilities needed in order to be able to learn any human language?

3. What is the relationship between the degree of diversity of human languages and the degree of complexity of innate abilities used in the acquisition of language?

The first two are general empirical questions and can only be given incomplete and tentative answers. We do not know exactly how different from one another human languages can be, first because we only have fragmentary descriptions of a few of the languages of the world, and second because actual human languages are not a random sample and therefore might not be a representative sample of all *possible* human languages. Similarly, the degree of complexity of the innate abilities involved in language acquisition is an open matter to be approached through empirical research and theoretical speculation.

On the other hand, a partial answer to the third question can be given on purely logical grounds. Consider two sets of languages, L and L' such that L is a proper subset of L' (i.e., all languages member of L are also members of L', while the converse is not the case). It does not matter for the argument what languages belong to L and L'. You may think of L as containing just English and of L' as containing just English and Chinese, or you may think of L as containing all the languages that humans could acquire according to a rationalist, and L' as containing all the languages that humans could acquire according to a relativist (remember that, for relativists, possible human languages are much more diverse than for rationalists).

Let us call A the least complex innate abilities sufficient for an organism to be capable of acquiring any language of L, and A' the least complex innate abilities sufficient for an organism to be capable of acquiring any language of L'. Now, either A and A' are equally complex or else A' is *more complex* than A. This is easy to prove: since L is a subset of L', A' constitutes sufficient innate abilities for an organism to be capable of acquiring any language of L. If innate abilities less complex than A' are not sufficient, then A' constitutes the least complex innate abilities sufficient for the acquisition of any language of L; in other words, in such a case, A is identical to A', and therefore cannot be more complex than it.

So, if the degree of complexity of innate abilities involved in language acquisition is at all affected by the degree of diversity of the languages to be acquired, then the relationship is a positive one: the greater the diversity, the greater the complexity. The acquisition of language and that of culture differ in many important respects (see Sperber 1975, chapter 4), but not with respect to the present argument: the greater the diversity of the cultures that humans are capable of acquiring, the greater the complexity of the innate learning abilities involved. Relativists might try to argue – quite implausibly – that there is no relationship between the two variables, but one thing they could not argue is that the relationship is an

43

inverse one (the greater the diversity, the lesser the complexity), that is they could not argue that evidence or arguments in favor of relativism weigh against innatism.

As one might have expected, no relativist model of cognitive development has ever been seriously worked out or even outlined. Cross-cultural psychology is generally not relativist.[6] Anthropological and philosophical relativists seem to have lost track of the development of psychology since the heyday of behaviorism. But one does not need a fully developed model to assess some of its difficulties and implications. A relativist model of development would have to represent a much more complex process and, everything else being equal, to rely more heavily on innatist hypotheses than a universalist model. The usual argument against universalism, that it implies unnecessary assumptions about innate mechanisms, should actually weigh – and quite heavily – against relativism.

Once the price is realized, the attraction of relativism should fade. But then anthropologists can ignore this price since it falls not on them but on psychologists (and psychologists also can ignore this price since they are not eager to buy relativism anyhow). If, however, we forgo the protection of interdisciplinary ignorance, we cannot remain happy relativists anymore. We have good reason now to take a second, hard look at the original evidence for relativism: how compelling is it? Is there really no alternative approach to the study of apparently irrational beliefs?

The evidence reconsidered

The evidence for relativism is twofold: studies of some alien categories show them to be culture-specific; interpretations of apparently irrational beliefs show them to "make sense" in the context of culture-specific world-views.

Suppose an anthropologist were to study contemporary British culture. Some of the words he would examine lend support to the view that meanings are culture-specific. They include:

a) Words the meaning of which involves (but is not exhausted by) definite reference to particular people, places, or times, e.g., "Marxism," "cockney," "Victorian."

b) Words with fuzzy meanings, e.g., "love," "faith," "leftism," "sport."

c) Words referring to socio-cultural institutions, e.g., "church," "doctorate," "debutante."

d) Words the definition of which is linked to an explicit norm or theory, e.g., "sin," "misdemeanor," "molecule," "Oedipus complex."

A considerable encyclopedic background is necessary to understand these words. Hence, in practice, they cannot be properly translated but at best rendered with much gloss and approximation.

44

Apparently irrational beliefs

The study of these words provides fairly strong evidence against the claim that meanings of all words except proper names are built up exclusively from a universal stock of basic concepts. On the other hand it provides only very weak evidence for relativism proper. The question indeed arises: do these words exhibit with particular clarity the true nature of meaning in general? Or are their culture-specific semantic properties peripheral additions to a universal stock? To answer this question, the evidence should come from a systematic study of whole lexicons, or, short of that, from the study of unfuzzy words lacking cultural salience. If these turn out to have thoroughly culture-specific meanings too, relativism would be vindicated.

Quite understandably, words without cultural salience have received little attention on the part of anthropologists. Recently, however, there have been systematic studies of various semantic fields such as color, botanical or zoological taxonomies (see Berlin 1978 for a review and discussion). Most of these studies do not corroborate a relativist view.

One striking example in this respect is the now famous study of basic color terms by Berlin and Kay (1969). Color terms were a favorite case for relativists: the color continuum was said to be partitioned freely, and hence most of the time differently, in each language. A more thorough and sophisticated study of the evidence shows, on the contrary, that a universal small stock of basic categories underlies superficial differences in terminology.[7]

This suggest a more general remark: relativists rightly insist that resemblances across cultures may well be superficial; failure to recognize this can lead to a false sense of understanding. Overlooked (except by structuralists) is the fact that cross-cultural differences may also be superficial, hence they provide no simple evidence for relativism.

Semantics is not a well-developed field, nor is meaning a well understood phenomenon. Cross-cultural semantic studies cannot be expected at this stage to provide conclusive evidence, although they tend to weigh against relativism (cf. Rosch 1974). We are left then with the indirect but allegedly decisive evidence provided by the study of apparently irrational beliefs.

It is a truism – but one worth keeping in mind – that beliefs cannot be observed. Ethnographers do not perceive that the people they study believe this or that; they infer it from what they hear and see. Their attributions of beliefs are therefore never uncontrovertible. Both the way in which the content of a belief is rendered and the description of the people's attitude as one of "belief" are open to challenge.

The content of a people's beliefs is inferred on the basis of translations of individual statements and speculations about the motives of individual or collective actions. These translations and speculations could in princi-

45

ple be discussed and evaluated. In most anthropological works, however, the reader is directly presented with an elaborate interpretation in the form of a consolidated, complex, and coherent discourse, with just occasional anecdotes and translations of native statements by way of illustration. Such interpretations are related to actual data in poorly understood, unsystematic and generally unspecified ways. They are constrained neither by standards of translation, nor by standards of description. They resemble the more indirect and freer forms of reported speech, where the utterances or thoughts reported can be condensed, expanded, coalesced, fragmented, pruned, grafted, and otherwise reworded at will.

Anthropological interpretations serve to convey part of the experience and the familiarity with an alien culture gained in the course of fieldwork. They are not primarily intended as evidence for factual or theoretical claims, and their use as such is limited and generally inconclusive.

It may well be that anthropological (and historical) literature suggests by its very bulk and drift that people of other cultures hold beliefs which are irrational by Western standards. It does not warrant, however, more specific or more explicit claims on the issue. In particular, no single properly spelled out proposition can be claimed to be believed by a given people. At best, the anthropologist may have grounds to suppose that a particular individual (e.g., Filate) holds some version of a particular belief (e.g., there are gold-hearted single-horned creatures), or that members of some group believe various propositions that resemble the anthropologist's rendering and one another.

Anthropological evidence does not warrant the assumption that particular beliefs are integrated into coherent, all-embracing culturally transmitted world-views. This assumption plays a major role in relativism. For relativists, the rationality of particular beliefs can only be assessed within the world-view to which they belong. Furthermore, there is no supracultural framework in which the rationality of the world-views themselves could ever be assessed.

Anthropological accounts of belief are usually written in the world-view format. But is this more than an expository device, a way to order and organize generally heterogeneous and scattered data? Godfrey Lienhardt, for instance, remarked in conclusion to his account of Shilluk cosmology:

Shilluk cosmological ideas . . . are not systematized by the people themselves, who reveal them only by their sayings and their behavior. It is impossible to give an account of them without abstracting them from the reality, formulating them as ideas with a certain degree of coherence between them, and thus constructing a system which has no exact counterpart in the thought of the Shilluk themselves (Lienhardt 1954: 162).

On the other hand, there are cases where the people themselves, or rather knowledgeable individuals such as the Dogon Ogotemmeli (Griaule

Apparently irrational beliefs

1948), the Hamar Baldambe (Lydall & Strecker 1979) or, in more complex societies, church-appointed specialists hold a systematic cosmological discourse. Thus the world-view format is not just the anthropologist's expository device. It can also be the native's. However, even the most elaborate cosmological discourse expresses only a small subset of the speaker's beliefs. Does this cultural discourse describe the cognizable world of the speaker? Or is it itself but an element of that world? This crucial question is not answered by the available anthropological evidence.

The assumption that culturally determined world-views constitute the general framework of people's beliefs is a psychological assumption and should be evaluated as such. It is about patterns of human cognition and, more specifically, about the organization of memory. This a domain where, at present, even the better worked out hypotheses remain highly speculative, and where available evidence is at best suggestive.[8] The fact that anthropologists find it feasible and useful to convey what they have understood of some people's beliefs in the form of an integrated discourse is suggestive too, but not more than, say, the fact that modern encyclopedias are organized in alphabetically ordered entries. Neither the discursive, nor the alphabetical order seem a very plausible model for the organization of memory, while both the idea of integration and that of autonomy of entries seem relevant but vague.

There is worse. A proposition can be paradoxical, counterintuitive or self-contradictory, but, in and by itself, it cannot be irrational. What can be rational or irrational is what one does with a proposition, for instance asserting it, denying it, entertaining it, using it as a premise in a logical derivation, etc. Thus, to decide whether some belief is rational we need to know not only its content but also in which sense it is "believed." Now, anthropologists do not use a technical concept of "belief" but the ordinary English notion, which does not correspond to any well-defined concept.

Clifford Geertz remarked:

Just what does "belief" mean in a religious context? Of all the problems surrounding attempts to conduct anthropological analyzes of religion this is the most troublesome and therefore the most often avoided (Geertz 1973: 109).

Rodney Needham, who has produced the only thorough anthropological discussion of the notion of belief, argued:

The notion of a state or capacity of belief . . . does not discriminate a distinct mode of consciousness, it has no logical claim to inclusion in a universal psychological vocabulary, and it is not a necessary institution for the conduct of social life. Belief does not constitute a natural resemblance among men (Needham 1972: 151).

Now, if the notion of "belief" used by anthropologists is at best vague and at worst empty, then reports of apparently irrational beliefs have little or no value as evidence for relativism.

47

At this point, a relativist might want to retort: "You are being unduly fussy. Anthropologists use 'belief' to refer objectively to what, from a subjective point of view, is just knowledge. When it is reported, for instance, that the Zande believe that there are witches, what is meant is that the Zande hold this as true just as they hold as true that there are cows, trees and stars. They would assert it or assent to it as a matter of course. How exactly should 'belief' be defined is for psychologists to discover. But even without a full characterization, some of the necessary conditions for a belief to be rational can be specified. A belief is not rational unless it is self-consistent and consistent with other beliefs held simultaneously. Now, many of the beliefs reported by anthropologists seem, by Western standards, to be self-contradictory or in contradiction with commonsense knowledge, hence irrational. This is the evidence for relativism. It may lack psychological polish and scientific precision, but these are no sufficient grounds to dismiss it."

The relativist's retort rests on one unwarranted empirical assumption, namely that religious and other apparently irrational beliefs are not distinguished from ordinary knowledge in the believer's mind (whether consciously or unconsciously).[9] It is generally harder to establish that something (here a psychological distinction) does not exist than to establish that it does. Even if the subjects failed to report a difference between their views on witches and their views on cows, even if they asserted both views in similar fashion, it would not follow that they hold them in the same way. Other tests might elicit a discrimination, whether a conscious or an unconscious one. Moreover, even the weak evidence provided by people's apparent behavior is generally lacking from works that assert the subjective equivalence of belief and knowledge. Most accounts of beliefs are written as if the utterances of so-called informants should all be taken on the same level, irrespective of whether they are produced in answer to the ethnographer's queries, during ordinary social intercourse, on ritual occasions, or during judicial proceedings. all native utterances are distilled together; their quintessence is than displayed as an homogeneous worldview in which, indeed, no epistemological differentiation of beliefs occurs. This, however, is a fact of ethnography, not of culture.

When a statement is aimed at informing, or when an idea is retained as part of one's knowledge, then consistency may well be a condition for rationality. However, the history of religious ideas, ethnographic studies of verbal behavior (e.g., Bauman & Sherzer 1974, Bloch 1975) and plain introspection strongly suggest that statements can be made with quite different purposes and with a great variety of degree and type of commitment, ideas can be entertained and held to be true in a variety of ways, criteria of rationality may vary with types of statements and classes of "beliefs."

Apparently irrational beliefs

Thus there are two ways of describing apparently irrational beliefs. According to the traditional description, their apparent irrationality comes from the fact that we initially assess them in the inappropriate framework of a modern Western world-view. According to the alternative description, they appear irrational because they are wrongly taken to belong to a class of "beliefs" for which consistency is a criterion of rationality. Anthropological literature is written *as if* the traditional description were correct, hence it provides no evidence for it. For all we know, the alternative description might be the correct one and this is enough to undermine the empirical basis of relativism.

Far from illuminating new areas and solving more problems than those which suggested its adoption in the first place, relativism, if taken seriously, would make ethnography either impossible or inexplicable, and psychology immensely difficult. It is the kind of theory any empirical scientist would rather do without. If, as I have argued, the evidence for relativism is weak and leaves us free to reject it, then we certainly should.

III. A RATIONALIST APPROACH

Propositional and semi-propositional representations

Relativism will not be given up merely on the ground that it is theoretically unappealing and empirically ill-supported. Is there, it will be asked, an alternative with greater explanatory power and better evidence in its favor? In *Rethinking Symbolism* (1975), I put forward what I believe is such an alternative. There, however, I was primarily concerned with establishing its superiority over various symbolist views. Here, I shall redevelop this rationalist approach in contrast to relativism.

"Believe" is standardly described as a verb of propositional attitude (Russell's phrase) along with "know," "suppose," "regret," "hope," etc. These verbs typically take as object a sentence introduced by "that" (e.g., "Paul assumes that Bill will come") and specify the mental attitude (here *assuming*) of the subject (*Paul*) to the proposition expressed by the sentential object (*Bill will come*). As already suggested, there is no reason to expect that these ordinary language notions would be retained by a well-developed psychological theory. But what of the more abstract notion of a propositional attitude? Is the problem just that "believe," "know," etc., provide too vague and arbitrary a classification for propositional attitudes, or is it, more radically, that there is no place in scientific psychology for a category of propositional attitudes at all, nor *a fortiori* for its sub-categories, however defined?

The recent development of cognitive psychology involves a shift back from the radical behaviorist rejection of all mental concepts to a more traditional view of the matter:

> Cognitive psychologists accept . . . the *facticity* of ascription of propositional attitudes to organisms and the consequent necessity of explaining how organisms come to have the attitudes to propositions they do.
> What is *un*traditional about the movement . . . is the account of propositional attitudes that it proposes: . . . having a propositional attitude is being in some *computational* relation to an internal representation (Fodor 1975: 198).

This framework for psychological research, to which, at present, there is no genuine alternative, is, however, neither without problems (see Dennett 1978, and Fodor himself) nor immune from revisions. I would like to suggest one emendation which, when it comes to the study of apparently irrational beliefs, has far-reaching consequences.

The phrase "propositional attitude" is misleading: it obscures the fact that we can have such "attitudes" to objects other than propositions in the strict sense. Propositions are either true or false. Sets of propositions are either consistent or inconsistent. Propositions, as opposed to sentences or utterances, cannot be ambiguous and hence true in some interpretations and false in others. Yet some of our so-called beliefs have several possible interpretations and we can hold them without committing ourselves to any of their interpretations.

A first example: Bob heard on the news

Stagflation has recently become the main problem of Western economies

and he "believes" it (as he would say himself). However Bob is not quite sure what "stagflation" means. What is it, then, that Bob believes? It could not be the proposition expressed by the journalist, since Bob is not capable of building the corresponding mental representation. It is not just the utterance, because Bob is capable of stating his belief by paraphrasing this utterance rather than merely quoting it; moreover, Bob believes many of its implications (e.g., that Western economies have a new important problem). There is, however, one expression that Bob cannot paraphrase and the implications of which he cannot compute, namely "stagflation." What Bob believes, then, seems to be a representation which combines several concepts with one unanalyzed or incompletely analyzed term.

Or consider, as a second example, the relativist slogan:

People of different cultures live in different worlds

I tried earlier on to fix its propositional content as charitably as I could, but the really charitable thing to do would have been to not to fix its content at all, which is the attitude of most relativists. They take for granted that this slogan literally expresses a true proposition, but finding out which proposition exactly, they see as an aim rather than as a precondition of relativist research. Relativists claim the right to select which of the apparent implications of their belief they will be committed to, and which of its apparent paraphrases they will acknowledge. This attitude is made easier by the vagueness of "different" and the fact that "worlds" in the plural has no fixed meaning at all in ordinary language. The object of the relativist belief, then, is neither a mere formula nor a real proposition: it is a conceptual representation without a fully fixed propositional content.

There are countless similar examples, which tend to show that the objects of our "propositional attitudes," the ideas we hold or otherwise entertain, are not always strictly propositional in character. Just as it would be mistaken to define "speaking" as "uttering *sentences*," it is mistaken, I suggest, to define thinking in terms of attitudes *to propositions*: many of our utterances do not match sentences but semi-grammatical strings; similarly, many of our thoughts are what we might call semi-propositional, they approximate but do not achieve propositionality. To express the same point more informally: if it were true that the objects of belief necessarily were propositions, then we could only believe ideas which we fully understand. I am arguing that we can also hold as beliefs incompletely understood ideas.

In order to clarify the notion of a semi-propositional representation, a comparison might be of help: a person's address is intended to identify one and only one domicile. To do so it must be complete. If, for instance, the street number is lacking, the domicile is approximately localized, but not fully identified. Similarly, the function of a conceptual representation is to identify one and only one proposition. However, it may fail to do so by being conceptually incomplete, i.e., by containing elements the conceptual content of which is not fully specified, in which case its function is not entirely fulfilled. A conceptual representation that succeeds in identifying one and only one proposition I shall call a *propositional representation*. It corresponds to a fully understood idea. A conceptual representation that fails to identify one and only one proposition, I shall call a *semi-propositional representation*.[10] It corresponds to a half-understood idea.

An address in which the street number is lacking can be completed in as many ways as there are numbers in the specified street: one of these ways must be the proper one. Similarly, a semi-propositional representation can be given as many *propositional interpretations* as there are ways of specifying the conceptual content of its elements (a half-understood idea can be made more precise in many ways). In principle, one of these interpretations is the proper one: it identifies the proposition to which the semi-propositional representation is intended to correspond. Suppose, for instance, that Bob thinks that stagflation means either *a stagnant infla-tion*, or *a combination of inflation and stagnation*, without being sure which; then the utterance 'stagflation has recently become the main prob-lem of Western economies' has two possible interpretations for Bob, one of which, he will assume, is the proper one, i.e., corresponds to the proposition that the journalist who produced the utterance was intending to convey.

Someone reluctant to accept the existence of semi-propositional repre-sentations might be tempted to attribute to Bob a belief with a proposi-tional content of the following disjunctive form:

Either a stagnant inflation, or a combination of inflation and stagnation has recently become the main problem of Western economies

This would not do, for two reasons. First, suppose that Bob later dis-covered that a stagnant inflation had become the main problem of West-ern economies, but, also, that the journalist had meant by stagflation "a combination of inflation and stagnation." If the content of Bob's belief had been the above disjunction, then he should feel the he had been right in his belief. But this, I take, is not what he would feel. Bob had believed what the journalist had said. What the journalist had said turned out to be wrong, and so did Bob's belief. The fact that a wrong propositional interpretation of what the journalist had said would make a true state-ment is irrelevant.

The second reason why half-understood ideas cannot be analyzed as disjunctions of all their possible propositional interpretations is that, in many cases (that of the relativist slogan for instance), the set of these disjuncts is fuzzy or undefined. In such cases, subjects would be unable to construct the appropriate disjunction. This could not be, therefore, a proper analysis of their belief.

Notice that some semi-propositional representation may in fact lack a "proper" interpretation. There is some utterance, say the relativist slo-gan, which I do not seem fully to comprehend; the best I can do is construct a semi-propositional representation of it. I imagine that one of the possible interpretations of this representation is the proper one, i.e., corresponds to the proposition that the speaker was trying to convey. However, the speaker might have uttered something which he himself does not understand so well, and of the content of which he too has a semi-propositional representation. If so, then, it is the semi-propositional representation that I have constructed, rather than any one of its proposi-tional interpretations, which corresponds to what the speaker actually intended to convey.

Why do we entertain semi-propositional representations? Is it just

52

some defectiveness of our cognitive system, or does it play a positive role? The latter, I shall argue.

Our capacity to form semi-propositional representations, i.e., to entertain an idea without fully understanding it, gives us the means to process information – and in particular verbal information – which exceeds our conceptual capacities. A semi-propositional representation enables us to store and process as much as we understand. It determines a range of possible propositional interpretations. Holding, moreover, that the proper interpretation has to be a true and a relevant one may help to select it on the basis of what was already known and what is thereafter learned. Thus a semi-propositional representation can serve as a step towards full comprehension. This, of course, is a common experience of childhood, when many lexical meanings are not fixed in our minds. It recurs throughout life in learning situations.

Inversely, if one finds oneself holding two mutually inconsistent ideas and is reluctant to give up either, there is a natural fall-back position. It consists in giving one of them a semi-propositional form. This occurs, for instance, in scientific thinking when counter-evidence causes the scientist, rather than rejecting the theory at stake, to search for a new interpretation of it by making some of its terms open to redefinition. As long as this search is going on, the theory is in a semi-propositional state.

Semi-propositional representations do not only serve as temporary steps towards or away from full propositional understanding. The range of interpretations and the search through that range, as determined by a semi-propositional representation, may be of greater value than any one of these interpretations in particular. The relativist slogan, the teaching of a Zen master, the philosophy of Kierkegaard, and, generally, poetic texts are cases to the point. Their content is semi-propositional from the start. The speaker's or author's intention is not to convey a specific proposition. It is to provide a range of possible interpretations, and to incite hearers or readers to search that range for the interpretations most relevant to them. The ideas that come as by-products of this search may suffice to make it worthwhile, particularly when no final interpretation is ever arrived at.

Well-behaved computers of today just turn down information which does not come in a required format. Human beings, on the other hand, need not be and cannot afford to be so choosy. Rather than reject information which they cannot represent propositionally, they try to salvage it by using semi-propositional representations. These play a role not only as temporary steps towards full propositionality but also as source of suggestion in creative thinking. This, I shall argue, is a crucial part of the psychological background against which the rationality of "beliefs" is to be assessed.

53

Factual beliefs and representational beliefs

In a cognitive framework, it is trivial to assume that the human system of internal representations (unlike, perhaps, that of other species) can serve as its own metalanguage; in other words, it allows for the representation of representations. From this assumption and the hardly less trivial assumption that conceptual representations can be propositional or semi-propositional, important consequences follow. To expound some of these consequences, I shall make a distinction between "factual beliefs" and "representational beliefs."[11]

From the point of view of the "believing" subject, factual beliefs are just plain "knowledge," while representational beliefs could be called "convictions," "persuasions," "opinions," "beliefs," and the like. In both cases what is being processed is a mental representation, but in the case of a factual belief there is awareness only of (what to the subject is) a fact, while in the case of a representational belief, there is an awareness of a commitment to a representation. Incidentally, to say that the way a subject is aware of his factual beliefs is different from the way in which he is aware of his representational beliefs, is not to say that the subject is aware *of the difference* between the two kinds of beliefs. In fact, I assume that most people are not aware of this difference (or else I would not be working at establishing it).

Let us assume (again, a trivial assumption in a cognitive framework) that a human mind contains an encyclopedic memory (i.e. a memory for conceptual representations, what most psychologists call, rather infelicitously, a "semantic" memory), and an inferential device which uses conceptual representations as premises and derives conceptual representations that logically follow from the premises.

We can now characterize factual beliefs:

A subject's factual beliefs are all the representations directly stored in his encyclopedic memory, and all the representations that, by means of his inferential device, he is capable of deriving from his stored representations.

Subjects don't have to label or mark their factual beliefs as "beliefs" or as "facts," or in any other way: they are factual beliefs by the mere fact of being stored in the right place or of being derivable from representations stored in the right place. For this kind of belief, you don't remember or compute that P is a fact or that you believe that P, you merely remember or compute that P.

Holding some factual belief commits you to believing also anything you are capable of inferring from it. This determines the rationality conditions for a factual belief. Holding a factual belief is rational when it is consistent with, and warranted by the other factual beliefs of the subject. However, making sure of the full consistency of factual beliefs is not a psychologically realistic goal. A plausible necessary condition, then, for rationally holding a factual belief is that it should have been matched and found consistent with all beliefs of closely related content, i.e., with those beliefs in the context of which it is likely to be relevant and which are most likely to provide evidence for or against it.

Given this, it can never be rational to hold a semi-propositional representation as a *factual* belief since some of the implications of its proper interpretation cannot be derived, and hence its consistency with related factual beliefs cannot be ascertained (leaving aside formal exceptions of no empirical import).

Factual beliefs are, we said, *directly* stored representations. The point is crucial because, given the meta-linguistic capacities of our system of internal representations, we can and do also have *indirectly* stored representations. These need not be factually believed, they can be entertained in all sorts of ways. For instance, the following ideas are somehow represented in my mind:

Hamlet saw the ghost of his father
A grammar is a model of a mental ability
There is no happiness without love

They are represented not directly but indirectly, i.e., they are embedded in a larger representation along the following lines:

In Shakespeare's play, Hamlet saw the ghost of his father
Chomsky has convincingly argued that a grammar is a model of a mental ability
It is commonly said that there is no happiness without love

To each of these embedded propositions, I hold a different attitude. That Hamlet saw his father's ghost, I take to be true in Shakespeare's play and false in our world. I would only assert it with reference to Shakespeare's play. That a grammar is a model of a mental device is an idea which I entertain favorably. I might, on occasion, assert it. However I don't take it to be a simple *fact*. I hold this view as a favored assumption, not as a factual belief. That there is no happiness without love, though not the kind of thing I would spontaneously utter, is nevertheless a view I might assent to in certain situations and in certain moods. It is far too vague to qualify as a fact in this or in any world, but it might on occasion serve to convey a relevant point.

So, in some everyday sense, I could be said to "believe" that a grammar is a model of a mental device or that here is no happiness without love. I believe these views not factually, but as a result of holding factual beliefs *about* them, I believe them, I propose to say, *representationally.*

Unlike factual beliefs, representational beliefs are a fuzzy set of related mental attitudes few of which seem to be universal. They could be characterized as follows:

A representation R *is a representational belief of a subject if and only if the subject holds some belief (factual or representational) about* R *such that he may sincerely state that* R.

Although a representational belief may be directly embedded in another representational belief, all representational beliefs must be directly or indirectly embedded in a factual belief: in the framework I am assuming, there is no other way for them to be mentally stored.

A representation R constitutes a paradigmatic case of representational belief when the subject holds a factual belief of the form:

the proper interpretation of R is true

When R is propositional, there is no difference in rationality between holding that the proper interpretation of R is true and holding that R. On the other hand, when R is semi-propositional, it may be quite rational to believe factually that the proper interpretation of R is true – and hence to believe R representationally – although it would be quite irrational to believe R factually.

What may make it rational to hold a representational belief of semi-propositional content is evidence on its source. Suppose I have plenty of evidence that my parents are truthful, and they tell me that the diviner is truthful but cryptic. Is it not rational, then, for me to believe factually that the diviner speaks the truth, to believe representationally what I understand him to say, and to interpret what he says in accordance with these beliefs? Or suppose that my teachers tell me that people of different cultures live in different worlds. It does sound silly. Yet my teachers could not be silly, could they? So, what they say must be profound. Profound: another word for semi-propositional.

One may be strongly committed to a representational belief of semi-propositional content, but then it is a strong commitment to a very weak claim. The wider the range of possible interpretations of R, the weaker the claim that its proper interpretation is true. Furthermore, rather than believing factually that the proper interpretation of R is true, the subject may, with similar results believe (factually or representationally) that:

R is what we were taught by wise people
R is a dogma of our Church
R is a holy mystery
R is deemed to be true
Marx (Freud, Wittgenstein . . .) has convincingly argued that R
Only heathens (fascists, people from the other side of the mountain . . .) would deny that R

Accepting any of these claims has little to do with the content of R and yet it would be enough to make the subject express R in an assertive form, invoke it freely, object to its being questioned, explore its possible interpretations, in short behave as a "believer."

Would we want to say, though, that in all these cases, the subject holds R as a representational belief? The question has less pertinence than it might seem, since, in any case, there is little reason to expect representational beliefs to constitute a well-defined class. They differ in this respect from factual beliefs. If humans have a capacity for factual beliefs, i.e., for constructing, storing, and deriving representations of facts, it is much more plausible that this capacity be part of the equipment which makes acquisition possible than that it be part of what is acquired. The same holds for the capacity to construct and process representations about representations. Once we have assumed this much, we have no need, and indeed we have no ground to further assume that there is a distinct innate capacity for entertaining representational beliefs.

An organism capable of holding all sorts of factual beliefs about representations can thereby develop or acquire an indefinite range of attitudes to representations extending (among other dimensions) from absolute commitment to absolute rejection. Dividing this range of what could be called "representational attitudes" into a few broad categories may be convenient, but there is no reason to expect these categories to have much psychological significance. "Representational beliefs" is such a category. How much should be included and where the line should be drawn is a matter of expediency rather than of truth.

For my present purpose, a broad category of representational beliefs, including all kinds of strong commitment to a representation, is the most convenient. It has the advantage of matching the anthropologists' own vagueness while clarifying what it is that they are being vague about. Anthropologists are vague as to what exactly is the attitude of the people to their beliefs, beyond its being one of commitment.[12] There is some justification for this vagueness, since there is no reason to assume that people expressing the same belief all have exactly the same attitude to it.

Anthropologists, then, use "belief" with a vagueness suited to their data. Philosophers discussing relativism (e.g., Lukes 1967) generally take for granted as a matter of mere definition that beliefs are "propositions accepted as true," i.e., in my terms that all beliefs are (or are logically equivalent to) factual beliefs.

With the two distinctions I have proposed, however, four classes of beliefs can be contrasted (see Table 1). Criteria of rationality differ for each of the four classes. Factual beliefs are rational to the extent that they can be assumed to be mutually consistent, with two consequences: factual beliefs must have been checked for mutual consistency at least in the

Table 1

	Factual Beliefs	*Representational Beliefs*
Propositional content	Strong criteria of rationality	Weak criteria of rationality
Semi-propositional content	Rationality impossible	Very weak criteria of rationality

context of closely related factual beliefs; factual beliefs of semi-propositional content, not being so checkable, are forever irrational. My guess is that humans of all cultures are quite successful in avoiding altogether factual beliefs of semi-propositional content (they are probably hardwired to filter them out), and are highly consistent in their factual beliefs of propositional content.

Representational beliefs are rational if they are the object of a rational factual belief which allows the believer to state them sincerely. This is clearly a weaker condition than the rationality condition for factual beliefs. Indeed it allows all factual beliefs to be also held as representational beliefs (i.e., to be held in a more reflexive, self-conscious manner), and of course it allows for further representational beliefs which could not qualify as rational factual beliefs. In the case of representational beliefs of propositional content (of which most scientific assumptions are good examples) their consistency with factual beliefs and other representational beliefs can be checked and provides reasons to hold or reject them, over and above the reasons already provided by factual beliefs about their source. In the case of representational beliefs of semi-propositional content, this check is not available, at least not to the same extent, and hence representational beliefs of semi-propositional content are the most easy ones to hold rationally.

Now, to which class of beliefs do the apparently irrational beliefs used as evidence for relativism belong?

If people of different cultures did hold apparently irrational *factual* beliefs, then it might be acceptable to try and reformulate the content of these beliefs so as to establish their rationality, even at the cost of having to imagine different cognizable worlds. But there is no reason, either theoretical or empirical, to assume that the apparently irrational beliefs reported by anthropologists and historians are factual beliefs. No theoretical reason: the very fact that, when assumed to be factual these beliefs appear irrational is reason enough to assume, on the contrary, that they are representational beliefs with a semi-propositional content, thereby avoiding the cost of relativism. No empirical reason: look in the literature for evidence as to the exact attitude people have toward their "beliefs;" what little evidence there is supports the view that the beliefs we are dealing with are representational and have a semi-propositional content.

That beliefs reported by anthropologists are representational is rather obvious: they are *cultural* beliefs, i.e., representations acquired through social communication and accepted on the ground of social affiliation. Anthropologists learn about these cultural beliefs by recording ritualized expressions of traditional wisdom, or by specifically questioning informants about the traditions of their people rather than about their own cogitations. So, what people take for a fact is the truth or the validity, the wisdom, the respectability, the orthodoxy, etc. of a representation, i.e., they believe this representation representationally.

Again that apparently irrational beliefs have a semi-propositional content is, to say the least, what the available evidence strongly suggests. In a few cases such as that of "mysteries" in the Catholic doctrine, the natives explicitly say so: the meaning (i.e., the proper propositional interpretation) is beyond human grasp. More often, the semi-propositional character of cultural beliefs is implicitly acknowledged in one of two ways. In some cases people offer exegeses of their beliefs, and, while sharing beliefs, wonder, argue or even fight about interpretation. In other cases, when you ask the people what their cultural beliefs mean, what they imply, how they fit with everyday facts, etc., they beg off, saying: "it is the tradition," "our ancestors knew" or something to that effect. Whether the proper interpretation is considered a secret lost or a secret to be discovered (or both), a clear if implicit distinction is made between holding a belief and knowing how to interpret it. This distinction only makes sense if these are semi-propositional beliefs.

This is not to say, obviously, that all culturally transmitted beliefs are semi-propositional. But then not all of them should appear irrational either. For instance, many culturally transmitted technical beliefs are rationally held factual beliefs or representational beliefs with a well-understood propositional content. More generally, I would expect that when culturally transmitted beliefs have a genuinely propositional content, whatever appearance of irrationality they may give can be dispelled by an intellectualist approach.

But aren't there counter-examples, evidence that apparently irrational beliefs (not explainable in intellectualist terms) are just facts to those who hold them? There are, at least, alleged counter-examples. Here is a well-known and typical one: Evans-Pritchard reported that the Nuer hold

that a twin is a bird as though it were an obvious fact, for Nuer are not saying that a twin is like a bird but that he is a bird (Evans-Pritchard 1956: 131).

But then Evans-Pritchard warns that we should not take Nuer statement about twins

> more literally than they make and understand them themselves. They are not saying that a twin has a beak, feathers, and so forth (ibid.).

Well, there is not such a thing as a non-literal fact. Hence if we pay close attention to the whole of Evans-Pritchard's report, we can no longer maintain that for the Nuer it is a fact that twins are birds. It is, rather, a commonplace representational belief of semi-propositional content. Generally speaking, when anthropologists assert that R is a fact for the So-and-So, their evidence is that the So-and-So tell and are told R without batting an eyelid. Hardly overstating the case, this is what all the evidence for relativism ultimately boils down to.

Anthropologists and philosophers have been carrying on only the semblance of a dialogue. Anthropological data does not have the easy theoretical relevance that relativism would endow it with. Relativism is a sophisticated solution to a problem which, as stated, does not even arise. If apparently irrational beliefs falsely appear to be irrational, it is not because their content is misrepresented, it is because in the first place they falsely appear to be beliefs in the philosopher's sense, i.e., propositions accepted as true. The problem is not one of poor translation (though, of course, poor translations are common), it is one of poor psychology.

I have suggested that we should make two psychological distinctions: between propositional and semi-propositional representations, and between factual and representational beliefs. Then all we need in order to dispel the appearance of irrationality of cultural beliefs is to establish that they are representational beliefs of semi-propositional content. Indeed, when all the members of your cultural group seem to hold a certain representational belief of semi-propositional content, this constitutes sufficiently rational ground for you to hold it too.[13]

That cultural beliefs are representational is almost tautologous; that they are semi-propositional is implicit and even sometimes explicit in the way people express and discuss them. There are many implications to this view of cultural beliefs (see Sperber 1975a, 1980) but only one concerns us here: relativism can be dispensed with.

Conclusion: beware of the dragon

And what about old Filate?

It may have been like this: one of the traders who come to Dorze on market days told him about the dragon. Was the trader in earnest? Where had he himself heard the story? It does not matter. Filate was enthralled. In his youth, he too had traveled and fought and hunted strange animals in the wilderness. Now he was too old, but he had to tell people. They would prepare, they would go. And when they came back with the trophy, they would thank him and include his name in their boasting songs.

Perhaps he had already taken his lyre and was about to give way to his emotion, as I had seen him do several times, singing himself to tears, when he realized what would actually happen: the people would not go, they would not sing, indeed, they would mock him. They would say: if a strange beast had been spotted, wouldn't we already have heard? No, if Filate had told them that he had seen, with his own gummy eyes, a stray wart hog on the path from Ochollo, they might have gone and looked. But he had been *told* that there was a dragon, *he* had been told . . .

Yet it had to be true. He felt it. He could bet on it. Such great news and no one would listen! Better keep quiet, he must have told himself dejectedly. But then it occured to him: the *forenj*, the white man who had arrived just a few months ago, he might listen. Yes, Filate now remembered, *forenj* went for big game, they even had special equipment. If anybody could kill a dragon, a *forenj* could. The *forenj* would be grateful. He would give Filate money and clothes.

And so he came to me.

What if I had expressed doubts that such an animal exists? He would have told me what he knew: they were golden all over; whether it was real gold or just the way they looked, he didn't know. Yes, their heart was of gold, real gold. How should he know if a heart of gold could beat? He was merely quoting what people who had killed these animals were reported to have said, and they knew better than any of us. Surely I must see that.

Though I will never know what really went on in Filate's head, I do not need to invoke a difference in cognizable worlds in order to conceive of plausible hypotheses.

What I eventually found more intriguing is the way in which I responded to Filate's request, and the fact that I left it out of my diary. Once I had understood that the old man was asking me to kill a dragon, my only worry became to turn down his request without hurting his feelings or appearing a coward.

"Kill a dragon!" I said, "I don't know if I could."

"What are you saying," he retorted angrily, "I thought *forenj* knew how to kill dragons."

"Oh well, yes, I see, yes, ah, but . . . I don't have a gun!"

"Couldn't you get one?"

I thought then of the French vet in the nearby town of Arba Minch. He might be interested and could procure a gun.

"Yes, I suppose I could get a gun. But I wouldn't know how to find the dragon. We *forenj* may be good at killing dragons, but not at tracking them."

This is when he said he would come back the next day, and left.

So, I had not managed to refuse, only to delay. But why in the first place had I been so eager to refuse? Was I afraid I would have to confront the dragon? Didn't I know that dragons don't exist? Sure I knew, but still . . .[14] I could have accepted without risk, I could have postponed the answer and asked appropriate ethnographic questions, but no, my purpose had been to extricate myself from a non-existent predicament, while, at the same time, toying with the idea of going ahead.

The next day, when reporting Filate's visit in my diary, I must have felt somewhat embarrassed, since I omitted the second half of the dialogue, the part that gives me away.

Thinking again about the episode (as I have done a few times over the years), I am now not so much puzzled by my response to Filate's request than by my embarrassment and my omission. Being asked to slay a dragon is a rare experience. It nevertheless evokes many childhood memories, fear and dreams. Why not, then, entertain the idea and enjoy it?

It must have been like this. There I was, a trained anthropologist on his first real field trip, and a native came and asked me to kill a dragon. In the first second I knew that I had hit on a great piece of data: a wise old man believing in an actual dragon, the cultural gap illustrated in a vignette! Yet, one second later, there I was, a reluctant dragon-killer staggering on the other side of the unbridgeable gap. At that point, the difference between Filate's thought processes and mine was that he knew how to enjoy them and make the pleasure last.

When I became my scholarly self again, taking scholarly notes, I recreated the alleged gap by conveniently omitting the embarrassing part of the episode, and I was left with a choice piece of evidence in favor of relativism.

The full story, then, is really a piece of evidence against relativism, but, more importantly, it is a piece of evidence *about* relativism. Several anthropologists (in particular Lévi-Strauss 1966, and Mary Douglas 1966) have stressed to what extent people will go in order to maintain or establish all kinds of conceptual gaps and boundaries between natural kinds, types of activity, the sexes, and, most important, between "us" and "them." In prerelativist anthropology, Westerners thought of themselves as superior to all other people. Relativism replaced this despicable hierarchical gap by a kind of cognitive apartheid. If we cannot be superior in the same world, let each people live in its own world.

The best evidence against relativism is, ultimately, the very activity of anthropologists, while the best evidence for relativism seems to be in the writings of anthropologists. How can that be? It seems that, in retracing their steps, anthropologists transform into unfathomable gaps the shallow and irregular boundaries that they had found not so difficult to cross, thereby protecting their own sense of identity, and providing their philosophical and lay audience with just what they want to hear.

3
Claude Lévi-Strauss today

No anthropologist has ever gained greater fame than Claude Lévi-Strauss, yet few have been more abstruse. In his case, both the fame and the abstruseness spring from common causes: the scale of the enterprise, its philosophical dimension, the poetic quality of his thought and his style of writing.

Most anthropologists devote themselves to the meticulous description of a single people. They limit their theoretical ambitions to the improvement of classifications or to short- or middle-range generalizations about "bridewealth" in Africa or "big-manship" in Melanesia. If challenged to spell out what they know about the human species in general, they will have little to say: that Homo sapiens is a viviparous biped that speaks and is endowed with superior learning abilities. Unsurprisingly, anthropologists are alone in showing some interest – but no enthusiasm – for the theoretical side of their work. As Edmund Leach remarked, Frazer and Malinowski became popular anthropologists because they were discussing sex or metaphysics, and so did, more recently, Margaret Mead and Castaneda. The case of Lévi-Strauss, who owes his fame to his theoretical writings, is truly exceptional.

Anthropologists' theoretical timidity is not wholly unjustified. When discussing "human nature" (to use the old phrase) it is hard to get away from platitudes without falling into arbitrariness or even absurdity. Moreover, it is unclear whether anthropologists are any better equipped for the task than, say, experimental psychologists. Indeed anthropologists' main contribution has been one of dissuasion. They have repeatedly shown that apparently natural aspects of human behavior are in fact cultural. Many anthropologists have even claimed that there is no such thing as a human nature, not realizing that they were thereby denying the very existence of a subject matter for anthropology.

Lévi-Strauss's innovation was to take hold of this dilemma by both horns: rather than treating human nature and cultural variability as two incompatible notions, he has attempted to show that the first lies behind the second as a unified, abstract structure governing concrete variations.

64

This principle is not new. It was taken for granted by classical philosophers of human nature. But they did not have to face the challenge of modern ethnographic knowledge. Lévi-Strauss set himself the task of renovating this principle, while at the same time meeting the challenge, by attempting simultaneously to make better sense of cultural peculiarities and to establish the intellectual unity of mankind. The task is a truly difficult one, calling for scientific creativity in a domain where scientific progress has hitherto been mostly destructive – of misconceptions. It seems unavoidable that Lévi-Strauss should introduce unconventional notions, maintain paradoxical hypotheses, appeal to vague intuitions, and experiment with sketchy models.

An important part of Lévi-Strauss's work is of a reflexive nature. In *Tristes Tropiques* (1955), a philosophical journey, in his *Conversations* with Georges Charbonnier (1961), in about half the essays in *Structural Anthropology* (1958) and *Anthropologie Structurale Deux* (1973), and in long passages in his other works, Lévi-Strauss considers the fate of anthropology and his own fate, advocates his "structural method," illustrating it with *ad hoc* examples, assesses the potential contribution of "structuralism" to other fields of inquiry, and points out its philosophical implications.

Understandably, these self-interpretive writings have been more widely read and discussed than those which deal directly with anthropological issues. Most praise and criticism has been directed at Lévi-Strauss's expositions of structuralism without anyone hardly ever wondering whether these expositions are an adequate account of his actual practice. That he might be wrong about the human species is obvious. That he might be wrong about his own work is usually not even considered. Yet in many respects, what Lévi-Strauss says about human nature is convincing, and what he says about his own work is disputable.

Take a marginal but characteristic instance. Lévi-Strauss asserts that all myths can be reduced to a canonic formula:

$$F_x(a) : F_y(b) :: F_x(b) : F_{a-1}(y)$$

In *Structural Anthropology* (1963a:225) he explains the formula in a short paragraph. In *From Honey to Ashes*, he mentions it again and adds: "It was necessary to quote it at least once more as proof of the fact that I have never ceased to be guided by it" (1973c:249). Should a chemist or a linguist make a similar claim, he would be expected to elaborate upon his formula beyond any risk of vagueness or ambiguity. Lévi-Strauss does nothing of the kind. He does not give a single step-by-step example. He does not even mention his formula anywhere else in his work. Most commentators have wisely pretended the formula did not exist.

There is no reason to doubt Lévi-Strauss's good faith; yet what on earth *is* he asserting? The answer is easy enough once one realizes that he tends to lump together his investigative strategy, his methodology, and his theory: the individual paths he happened to follow, the shared ground rules of scholarship, and the general assumptions he has arrived at. When he claims that he has "never ceased to be guided" by his formula, he sounds not like a scientist but rather like a transcendental meditator claiming to be guided by his mantra.[1] This is an autobiographical fact which there is little reason either to question or to emulate.

Similarly, when in *Tristes Tropiques* Lévi-Strauss talks of geology, Marxism and psychoanalysis as his "three mistresses" ("three sources of inspiration" in the most recent English translation), he is describing how his ideas took shape, not what they are. In more conventional thinkers, there may be a quite straightforward relation between the two, but not with Lévi-Strauss, who has an extraordinary ability to perceive and exploit the most indirect relationship. Thus in his case direct inspiration may have been less determinant than a perception of the potential fruitfulness of developing views symmetrically opposed to those of the then influential philosopher Henri Bergson, by stressing discontinuity rather than continuity, intellect rather than emotion.[2]

Lévi-Strauss is both a scholar and an artist. His choice of topics, examples, references, and points of comparison is of a highly unconventional eclecticism. The indexes to his books read like surrealistic inventories: ". . . Manioc, Marriage, Mars (planet), Marsupials and marsupial pouch, Martin de Nantes, Masters of honey, Mato Grosso, Maundy Thursday, Melanesia, Menstruation, Meta-linguistic devices. . ." The relation which the illustrations bear to his text is often to be guessed at. The title and organization of chapters in his books on myths suggest a musical composition rather than a work of scholarship, with an "overture," and a "finale," and "sonata," "fugue," "cantata," "symphony," "variations," etc. along the way. The whole work is dedicated "To Music." The first epigraph is a line from a song, given with the score. The explanation of all this is to be found in the *finale*: Lévi-Strauss suggests that modern music from Frescobaldi and Bach onwards was the heir of myth; after Wagner, musicians renounced this legacy and structural analysis took it over:

Only one alternative was left to music: to get rid of mythical structures which then became available for myth at last to reach self-awareness in the shape of a discourse on itself [i.e. Lévi-Strauss's own work!] (1971:584).

Lévi-Strauss's use of figures of speech is truly original (and sometimes disconcerting). With most writers, concrete metaphors, allegories or examples tend to be used to illustrate or express more abstract ideas. Lévi-Strauss's imagination often runs the other way round. He has a special taste for abstract, formal figures of speech (which his readers too often confuse with actual abstraction and formalism).

One of his favorite figures is a fairly rare form of "abstract for concrete" substitution or synecdoche whereby a quality is used as an equivalent for the person of thing which possesses it: a calabash is referred to as a "container," the beverage in it as the "contained." A moccasin is a "cultural object," grass a "natural object." Less trivially, bone is referred to as "the reverse of food," a thornbush as "nature hostile to man," a moccasin again as "anti-land," and so on. When, on a rare occasion, Lévi-Strauss uses a concrete, everyday metaphor, and compares a system of symbolic classification to a "utensil with crossed metal blades which is used for cutting potatoes into slices or chips," he immediately redescribes the utensil in wholly abstract terms:

A "preconceived" grid is applied to all the empirical situations with which it has sufficient affinities for the elements obtained always to preserve certain general properties (1966:149).

These abstract synecdoche become the instruments of a second favorite figure of speech: antithesis. A container is contrasted with a contained, a cultural object with a natural one, etc. The more elaborate synecdoches enable the antithesis to be further developed into a chiasmus, or "symmetrical inversion" in Lévi-Strauss's terms. Here is an excellent specimen of the kind (he is talking about Western, more specifically French, cultural images of domestic animals):

If birds are *metaphorical human beings* and dogs *metonymical human beings*, cattle may be thought of as *metonymical inhuman beings* and racehorses as *metaphorical inhuman beings* (1966:207)

These peculiar figures of speech are used by Lévi-Strauss at two levels: in analyzing cultural categories (as in the examples above), or in reflecting upon anthropological notions. While, at the first level, this can often be illuminating, at the second, reflexive level, it tends to be a source of confusion. Take a typical instance; Lévi-Strauss claims we should regard:

marriage regulations and kinship systems as a kind of language, a set of processes permitting the establishment between individuals and groups, of a certain type of communication. That the mediating factor, in this case, should be the *women of the group*, who are *circulated* between clans, lineages, or families, in place of the *words of the group*, which are *circulated* between individuals, does not at all change the fact that the essential aspect of the phenomenon is identical in both cases (1963a:60).

How is this striking conclusion arrived at? First, by means of two abstract synecdoches, marriage regulations and kinship systems are reduced to the circulation of women, and spoken language is reduced to the circulation of words. Second, by a "species for genus" synecdoche, all kinds of circulation are equated to one special form of it, namely communication. Third, by another similar synecdoche, communication is equated to one of its special forms: language (understood as a general abstract category).

Each of these steps is open to objection.

Marriage and kinship involve much more than the circulation of women: they involve the organization of corporate groups, conventional attitudes and expectations, the circulation of various kinds of goods, the transmission of rights, property and knowledge, and so on. Lévi-Strauss however has devoted a whole book (*The Elementary Structures of Kinship*) to arguing that the circulation of women *is* the "central aspect" of kinship.

On the other hand, the innocent-looking assertion that the circulation of words is the essential aspect of language is smuggled in. In Saussurian terms, the way in which words circulate is an aspect of *parole* and not of *langue*; or in Chomskyan terms it is an aspect of linguistic performance and not of competence . The structure of spoken language determines not who says what to whom, but what can be said at all in a given tongue, irrespective of who the interlocutors are. A language is a *code* which determines which messages are available for (among other possible uses) circulation in the social network to which the interlocutors belong. By contrast, a marriage system is a *network*, whose structure determines which channels between social groups are open to the "circulation of women." Women are made available not by any kind of code, but through biological reproduction. So, even if one accepts the notion that both spoken language and kinship are communication systems, the "essential aspect" of one is a code and of the other a network, two very different kinds of structures.

In any case, to equate circulation and communication is also objectionable. If words circulate between you and me, communication is indeed taking place: at the end of the verbal exchange, we both possess – and therefore we share – all the information that has been conveyed. On the other hand, if we exchange my cow for your horse, the animals have been circulated, they have not been communicated. At the end of the process we need have no more in common than we had at the start.

Nor should it be taken for granted that "a set of processes permitting the establishment between individuals and groups, of a certain type of communication" is necessarily "a kind of language." Information can be transmitted in two ways: either by coding it in a shared language or by bringing attention to it, by making it manifest. For instance, if I am told to go, I can say "I refuse to go," or I can behave in a way which makes it manifest that I refuse to go; either way I succeed in transmitting the information. Most human communication involves a mixture of these two forms. Now if we accept, for the sake of argument, Lévi-Strauss's notion that women are the messages communicated in a kinship system, surely these messages consist of information made manifest rather than of coded information; they are not in any sense "linguistic."

Thus the assertion that a kinship system is a language can only be analyzed as a complex metaphor based on questionable synecdoches. The greater part of Lévi-Strauss's work is more modest, more painstaking and much more relevant to anthropological understanding and knowledge, even though his style remains a baroque combination of order and fantasy.

Besides *Tristes Tropiques* and the papers collected in *Structural Anthropology* and *Anthropologie Structurale Deux*, Lévi-Strauss's work falls into three groups. First, his doctoral dissertation, *The Elementary Structures of Kinship* published in 1949, revised in 1967, and published in English in 1969, which has been a source of much controversy. Second, two books, *Totemism* and *The Savage Mind* (both originally published in 1962) on the classificatory activities of the human mind, the theme most central to his work. Third, the four volumes of his *Introduction to a Science of Mythology* (in French, more elegantly, *Mythologiques*): *The Raw and the Cooked* (1964), *From Honey to Ashes* (1966), *The Origin of Table Manners* (1968), *L'Homme Nu* (1971).

My aim is not to summarize these works but to consider selected themes and issues, without following chronological order, or trying to be exhaustive. For Lévi-Strauss, all his work is a defense and illustration of the structuralist method. Indeed it is hard to say which of Lévi-Strauss or structuralism has made the other famous. But, I shall argue, structuralism has become an uninspiring frame for an otherwise stimulating and inspired picture.

Untamed thinking

At the very beginning of *The Savage Mind*, Lévi-Strauss argues against the notion that "primitive" people are incapable of abstract thought. Most anthropologists would agree with him and cite as evidence the highly varied and elaborate moral and metaphysical notions which they have found and studied all around the world. Lévi-Strauss is fully aware of these notions; he has himself analyzed several, for instance those of *mana* and *hau* in his "Introduction to the Work of Marcel Mauss." Instead of these obvious cases, he chooses as evidence the Chinook language of the American Northwest, in which a proposition such as "the bad man killed the poor child" is said to be rendered: "the man's badness killed the child's poverty." Thus for Lévi-Strauss, the epitome of "primitive" abstraction seems to be abstract synecdoche, his own favorite figure of speech! Perhaps this is not the best piece of evidence, but it is certainly the most revealing of Lévi-Strauss's own turn of mind. This peculiar turn of mind is a source of incomparable insights into the underlying structure of folk classifications and folk narratives.

On anthropological knowledge

There is an interesting relationship between Lévi-Strauss's way of thinking and that of the people who tell myths. It is one not of similarity but of complementarity: Lévi-Strauss tends to represent a concrete object by one of its abstract properties; this makes him particularly apt at unraveling the thought of people who tend, on the contrary, to represent an abstract property by some concrete object which possesses it, i.e. people given to using a "concrete for abstract" form of synecdoche.

In traditional cultures, abstractions such as moral qualities are often depicted concretely, in the guise of animal characters for instance. This is a fact known not only to anthropologists but often also to the natives themselves, and, actually, the same device is at work in modern culture too. If Lévi-Strauss's contribution had been merely to stress and illustrate this fact, he would be only one in a long line of scholars who, since antiquity, have been disputing whether fables are allegories based on metaphorical or synecdochical relationships, and what entities or notions they represent. At the end of the nineteenth century, for instance, followers of Max Muller argued that myths were allegories of the sun and of solar manifestations, against the followers of Adalbert Kuhn, who favored thunder and storms. More recently the French mythologist Georges Dumézil has put forward a synecdochical interpretation of Indo-European myths and rituals: through their characters and actions, they represent, he claims, three basic social "functions:" sovereignty, war, and fertility.

Lévi-Strauss's approach is original in three ways.[3] Firstly, in its purpose: what he aims at understanding through the study of cultural symbolism is neither some primitive stage in human intellectual development nor the underlying ideology of a specific cultural area, but a mode of thinking shared by all humans, irrespective of time and place. Secondly, he is not concerned with ascribing a single interpretation to each symbol, but rather with showing that symbols are open to a great variety of different and complementary interpretations. Thirdly, he is concerned with systematic relationships between symbols; the abstract level of interpretation is a means of establishing these relationships rather than an end in itself.

The translation of the French title *La Pensée Sauvage* by *The Savage Mind* gives a false idea of Lévi-Strauss's general purpose. It suggests that there may be other kinds of human mind besides the "savage" one, when in fact Lévi-Strauss has been one of the most systematic critics of this view in all its many guises. Since the book is about intellectual processes rather than their product, *pensée* should be translated as "thinking" rather than "mind" or "thought." *Sauvage* has three standard translations: "savage," "wild," and "untamed." But Lévi-Strauss warns us that he does not mean *la pensée des sauvages* (the thinking of savages); for

70

him *la pensée sauvage* is simply human thinking as long as it is not submitted to explicit rules or aided by techniques such as writing or advanced calculus. It is not contrasted with civilized thinking – all human thinking is civilized – but with a way of thinking that has been domesticated, tamed in order to increase the quality or at least the quantity of its output. In this respect "untamed thinking" best conveys the sense of the French title: it makes it clear that there are not two types of mind but only one – which can be trained and put to particular uses (such as modern scientific investigation).

Much can be learned about human thinking in general by observing and experimenting upon members of our own society. Nevertheless, by ignoring untamed thinking and its products, one risks bypassing abilities hampered or obscured by domestication. Besides being interesting ethnographically, the study of societies which lack writing has a general psychological relevance: in them, intellectual mechanisms operate unaided by artificial memory, and unguided by formal teaching. It is not that members of those societies are any closer to human nature: each and every one of us is as close to human nature as it is possible to be. It is that the products of natural abilities are less confused with those of artificial devices.

Here, Lévi-Strauss's approach can be contrasted with the two basic views which each in turn have dominated anthropology. Not so long ago, exotic peoples were thought to be psychologically different from ourselves, so that to study them was of psychological relevance from both an evolutionary and a comparative point of view. More recently, the psychic unity of humankind has been generally recognized and used as an argument to separate anthropology from psychology: since the human mind is everywhere the same, anthropologists should not burden themselves with a study that can be carried out in salubrious laboratories. Lévi-Strauss's originality in this respect, which has often gone unnoticed or been misunderstood, is to have developed this notion of the psychic unity of humankind while, at the same time, putting forward new arguments to show that ethnography has a true, indeed unique, psychological relevance.

The "proper" interpetation of symbols is a pursuit long practiced in the West. In medieval hermeneutics, it has a strongly normative character; in modern anthropology and comparative religion, it purports to be strictly descriptive. But the mere idea that there is or can be a "proper" interpretation for symbols is itself normative, when in most societies individuals are left fairly free to interpret symbols as they please. If the scholar's purpose is to throw light on what people do think rather than what they should think, then the classical approach needs to be revised.

Lévi-Strauss has undertaken such a revision and developed an alternative to the various rival methods of deciphering symbols. But, once again, the way he describes his approach can be misleading. Faithful to the

71

terminology of Saussure, he tends to refer to symbolic phenomena as "signifiers," and one might assume that the investigation is into an underlying code which pairs these signifiers with their "signifieds." Yet, if readers begin looking for the signifieds, they soon realize that the underlying code relates signifiers to other signifiers: there *are* no signifieds. Everything is meaningful, nothing is meant.

What Lévi-Strauss actually does is neither to decipher symbols nor to describe a symbolic code. Rather, he attempts to show in what ways natural and social phenomena lend themselves to intellectual elaboration, what selection of features this involves, and what kind of mental associations can thus be established.

Any object in the world has an indefinite number of features. Only some of these ever attract our attention and even fewer do so when we attend to the object with some special aim in mind. Thus different features of an animal, say, will be taken into consideration depending on whether we are concerned to know to which taxonomic category it belongs, whether it is edible, whether it is dangerous, whether it is worth photographing. It is often claimed that the concerns of technologically primitive people are overwhelmingly practical, and one would therefore expect them to pay almost exclusive attention to such features in animals as edibility or the danger they represent to humans. But this is very far from being the case. Modern scientific or technical thinking pays attention to features selected according to strict criteria of relevance. But "untamed" thinking seems to be indifferent to relevance, or rather to have a much wider notion of it. Thus, contrary to expectation, most peoples in the world pay more attention to aspect such as what animals eat rather than to which animals can be eaten.

Many pages of *The Savage Mind* are devoted to illustrating the endless variety of interest which humans everywhere take in their environment. The Navajo Indians, for example, are concerned with the way in which animals move; they classify them according to such features as whether they run, fly, or crawl; whether they travel by land or by water; whether they travel by day or by night. For the Ojibwa Indians, a relevant feature of the squirrel is that it inhabits cedar trees; the Fang of the Gabon are concerned with the fact that squirrels take shelter in the holes of trees, rather than with the species of the tree.

The Asmat of New Guinea have yet another point of view:

Parrots and squirrels are famous fruit-eaters . . . and men about to go headhunting feel a relationship to these beings and call themselves their brothers . . . (because of the) parallelism between the human body and a tree, the human head and its fruits (Zegwaard 1959, quoted in Lévi-Strauss 1966: 61).

For Westerners the comparison between the human head and fruit would, as a matter of course, be based on shape, and the analogy according to which heads are to bodies what fruits are to trees would seem superfluous and contrived. This is not so for the Asmat, as we discover in Zegwaard's article. From a headhunter's point of view, heads are a detachable and valuable upper appendage of the body, a relationship analogous to that between fruit and tree, as seen by fruit-eaters. Moreover, The Asmat would eat ritually the victim's brain, and they would point out that "the human head also has a hard shell which protects the core like a coconut."

Since any object has an indefinite number of features, it can enter into an indefinite number of associations with other objects. A given culture may highlight some of these features and associations, while the other remain merely potential. Although they are not spelled out, some of these extra associations may be strongly suggested by the structure of myth or ritual; others may be brought into play by creative individuals who add to ritual rules or transform myths in the course of transmitting them. Given this, the anthropologist should not only record the explicit associations of standard symbols but also pay attention to the culturally salient features of a much wider range of phenomena.

In traditional "keys" to symbols, whether popular or scholarly, items are considered one by one and each is given its proper interpretation either by fiat or according to some preconceived notion of what the symbol *must* mean. But when attempting an unprejudiced description, there is no way of deciding, for each item separately, which of its many features would be salient in a given culture. If, instead, relationships between items are considered, then shared or contrasted features stand out as the basis for symbolic associations. The greater the number of items taken into consideration, the fewer the features which are likely to play a role: one should not study symbols but symbolic systems.

It is by thus looking for systems of relationships that Lévi-Strauss came to take a new interest in an old anthropological question, that of totemism. His short book, *Totemism*, and the chapters on this topic in *The Savage Mind* provide an excellent illustration of this aspect of his work.

By "totemism" we usually mean a combination of features: a belief in a special relationship between an animal or plant (called the totem) on the one hand and a human group on the other; prohibitions in the relationships of humans to their totem; special rituals; and sometimes also a belief that the totem is the ancestor of the group, totemic group exogamy, etc. At the end of the nineteenth and at the beginning of the twentieth centuries, totemism was much discussed; it was believed by some anthropologists to be the source of religion, by most to be a stage in human evolution. However, almost from the start, a few authors questioned the homogeneity of totemism and saw it either as an ill-defined part of a wider phenomenon, or as the illegitimate lumping together of independent features. Lévi-Strauss develops both criticisms: For him, "totemism" denotes the contingent co-occurrence of sundry manifestations of a general human propensity to classify. Anthropologists have tended to lose interest in what hey saw as an inadequate notion, but by the same token they have ceased to pay sufficient attention to the forms of classification totemism was intended to encompass. Lévi-Strauss's aim is to reconsider these classifications from a different point of view.

If the question asked were: "Why should a given social group consider itself to stand in a special relationship to, say, eagles?," only unsatisfactory answers could be given: "Because they are mistaken about their ancestry," or "because they think they resemble eagles and assume this implies a relationship." Explaining strange behavior by even stranger intellectual errors is no explanation at all.

The question could be reframed: "Why should a society consider that each of its constituent groups stands in a special relationship to a different species of animals?" Now it is the whole set – and not just one – of the dyadic relationships between social groups and animal species that is taken into account. This opens up a choice of perspectives: the overall picture can be redrawn as a single dyadic relationship between the two sets: of social groups and animal species. Animals can now be considered as emblems or proper names used to individuate human groups. The social set is mapped onto the animal set. This is the beginning of an explanation but it is not yet sufficient. If this were all, why not use arbitrary names? Why so much content when pure form would do just as well?

Lévi-Strauss points out that the human-animal relationship can be understood in a third, even more systematic way: neither as a set of dyadic relationships between individual items, nor as a dyadic relationship between sets of individual items, but as a second-degree dyadic relationship between two sets of first-degree relationships:

On the one hand there are animals which differ from each other (in that they belong to distinct species, each of which has its own physical appearance and mode of life), and on the other hand there are men . . . who also differ from each other (in that they are distributed among different segments of the society, each occupying a particular position in the social structure). The resemblance presupposed by so-called totemic representations is *between these two systems of differences* (Lévi-Strauss 1963b: 77).

Seen in this light, the recourse to animal species provides a unique system of differences. Species do not overlap, they look different, they live differently, they offer an endless choice of opposed features that can be used to contrast human groups.

"Totemic" beliefs and rituals may highlight some of these features. For instance:

The folllwing clans stand in a joking relationship to each other among the Luapula (of Zambia): the Leopard and the Goat clans, because the leopards eat goats, the Mushroom and the Anthill because mushrooms grow on anthills, the Mush and Goat clans because men like meat in their mush, the Elephant and the Clay clans because women in the old days used to carve out elephants' footprints from the ground and use these natural shapes as receptacles instead of fashioning pots (Lévi-Strauss 1966: 62).

Here the joking relationship between clans is based on specific features of the relationship between totems. Formal proper names could not be exploited in this way. Indeed, in such a case, form and content cannot be dissociated.

Even without such explicit elaborations, the system may render salient certain implicit features. If, for instance, a tribe were divided into three clans named after the eagle, the bear, and the turtle, this might suggest that we concentrate on the natural element of each of these species, and further contrast the three clans as associated with sky, earth and water.

It might seem that the system of differences among animal species is too powerful to match the much weaker differences among human groups. Members of the same society look alike and live in similar ways and conditions; social groups do not differ in the way natural species do. But the point precisely is that human groups are trying through "totemic" institutions not to match two preexisting systems of differences, but rather to build one system with the help of the other. They are trying not so much to *express* social differences as to create or strengthen them. In this respect the force of the animal system is never excessive. Whatever aspects of it can be mapped onto the social system are welcome.

Thus understood, the symbolic potential of "totemic" animals appears both systematic and open-ended. There can be no question of ascribing a proper interpretation to each animal: on the one hand these animals cannot be interpreted outside of their mutual relationships; on the other hand new relationships, and hence new interpretations, are always possible.

This Lévi-Straussian account of totemism depends, however, on certain psychological assumptions. Earlier accounts assumed that human beings make intellectual mistakes, or that they have a use for for naming systems. Neither assumption is extravagant. Lévi-Strauss further assumes that the human mind is able and liable to impose a specific kind of organization on its representation of the world. This departs from the strict empiricist view of learning prevalent in modern anthropology, and expectable objections have cropped up. I would argue that we should depart even more from the empiricist *a priori* (see Sperber 1974) and go further in the rationalist direction in which Lévi-Strauss has made a first step.

Shouldn't we, for instance, make a sharp distinction between encyclopedic classifications such as folk taxonomies of the fauna or flora, and symbolic classifications such as "totemism?" Encyclopedic classifications aim at *registering* observable differences and resemblances, and they can be challenged on empirical grounds. Taking advantage of encyclopedic classifications, symbolic classifications aim at *instituting* differences and resemblances. They do not obey the same constraints. They involve a specific form of creativity (see Sperber 1975b). Lévi-Strauss gives too much importance to the fact that in both cases the end-product is a classification. He fails to appreciate the differences in the intellectual processes involved. He does not contemplate the further psychological assumptions which are required in order to account for these differences.

Even so, Lévi-Strauss's approach to totemism has radically renewed the issues. Lévi-Strauss assumes that the structure of such symbolic systems as totemic classification is determined by a universal human ability rather than by the alleged inability of "primitives" to think in abstract terms, or by practical need, whether individual or social. He neatly summarizes this when he says that symbolic animals are chosen not because they are "good to eat," but because they are "good to think" – not, that is, because they are food but because they are food for thought.

Imagine a fossil organism about whose digestive system we knew nothing. If we had the good fortune to discover that a specific range of foodstuffs had been optimal for it, we could then make assumptions about that digestive system. Now, if Lévi-Strauss is right and cultural symbols such as totems are optimal food for thought, then their study offers a new approach to the study of the human mind. Conversely the study of the human mind can throw new light on cultural symbolism. The use Lévi-Strauss makes of these new perspectives is stimulating rather than convincing, but this matters less than the fact of having opened them up.

Myth

The four volumes of *Mythologiques* are a monumental illustration and development of the central idea in *The Savage Mind*: that concrete categories can serve as intellectual tools to express abstract notions and relationships; and that "untamed" thinking tends to order its world in this way.

Most cultural phenomena, such as technology or political organization, must submit to a variety of ecological and sociological constraints. By contrast, myths – orally transmitted and culturally selected narratives – tend to ignore any determination other than cultural ones. Hence the study of myths should provide a direct insight into the spontaneous working of the human mind. To expand on this premise, Lévi-Strauss reviews in *Mythologiques* more than eight hundred American Indian myths and a wealth of other ethnographic data. Each myth is considered in relation to many others. The resulting web is too intricate to isolate one fragment. Rather, in order to illustrate Lévi-Strauss's approach and to develop certain criticisms of it, I shall start from a much shorter and more modest text, a paper entitled "Four Winnebago Myths: A Structural Sketch" (Lévi-Strauss 1960).

The American anthropologist Paul Radin published together four myths which he had collected among the Winnebago Indians (Radin 1949). Lévi-Strauss's aim is to show that these myths were even more closely related to each other than Radin himself had realized. The argument concerns most particularly the fourth myth which, to Radin, appeared quite atypical. Indeed, at first sight, it seems not to belong with the three others at all. Here is my summary of this fourth myth:[4]

An orphan boy, a good hunter like his father, lived with his grandmother at the end of the village. The daughter of the village chief saw him and fell in love with him: "would that he would take liberties with me or that he would say a word to me or court me." This is what she earnestly desired, indeed this she constantly thought of. The boy was still somewhat immature and never said a word to her. She did not dare speak and after a long time spent in unhappy yearning, she fell ill and died. On top of her grave, dirt was piled so that nothing could seep through.

Out of grief, the chief decided to move with all the villagers to a place several days' journey away. The orphan boy, however, did not want to go for fear that the hunting would not be as good there. With the permission of the chief, he and his grandmother stayed behind to take care of the chief's daughter's grave. Before leaving, the chief had the floor of their lodge covered with dirt to keep it warm.

The orphan, who could "not yet pack animals very far," hunted in the vicinity, avoiding the old village. One evening, having chased his wounded quarry further than usual and returning late, he crossed the village and noticed a light in the old chief's house. Inside he saw the chief's daughter's ghost. She told him what had caused her to die, and added: "because of thus behaving, I am dead, but my ghost has not yet departed to the place where the ghosts go. I beseech you, try to help me this time." To bring her back to life, she told him, he would have to submit to a test: he must spend four nights in the chief's house. Each night he must try to fight off sleep by telling stories in front of a big fire. When he felt too sleepy and lay down, "you will have the sensation as though something was crawling over your body; but they will not be insects doing it. Do not under any condition grab for the place itching." Although each night it was more difficult, the orphan boy succeeded in passing the test. The ghosts who had been torturing him let him go, and he was able to restore the girl to life, to bring her to his house and to marry her

Having heard the news, the villagers returned. The young wife son gave birth to a boy. "Now when the boy was able to shoot real arrows, then the husband spoke to his wife and said, 'Although I am not yet old, I have been on earth as long as I can . . . However, I shall not die as you did; I shall simply go home, just so.' " She chose to go with him, and they both became wolves and lived under the earth. Sometimes they come back to this earth to bless an Indian when he fasts.

As is often the case with myths, the episodes here seem to follow each other without really following *from* each other. The causal links are weak. Many details (many more in the full text) seem unnecessary. My-thologists tended to think that myths were indeed loosely organized and consisted largely of in ornamental flourishes. Against this, Lévi-Strauss argues that there is more structure to a myth than the mere succession of episodes. There is a whole system of correspondences among the ele-ments of the myth, over and above their chronological order.

Thus in this particular myth, the orphan boy and the chief's daughter are at opposite ends of the *social* scale. The relationship is reversed though, argues Lévi-Strauss, when *natural* abilities are considered: the girl is "paralyzed when it comes to expressing her feelings"; she is a "defective human being, lacking an essential attribute of life." The boy, on the other hand is "a miraculous hunter, i.e., he entertains privileged relations with the natural world, the world of animals."

Therefore we may claim that the myth actually confronts us with a polar system consisting of two individuals, one male, the other female, and both exceptional in so far as each of them is overgifted in one way and undergifted in the other . . . The plot consists in carrying this disequilibrium to its logical extreme; the girl dies a *natural* death, the boy stays alone, i.e. he also dies but in *social* way . . . Their positions are inverted: the girl is below (in her grave), the boy above (in his lodge) (Lévi-Strauss 1960: 358).

This last opposition is confirmed by the apparently superfluous detail of dirt being piled on the grave in one case, and on the floor of the lodge in the other, which "emphasizes that, relative to the earth surface, i.e., dirt, the boy is now above and the girl below."

This new equilibrium, however, will be no more lasting than the first. *She who was unable to live cannot die; her ghost lingers "on earth"* . . . *With a wonderful symmetry, the boy will meet a few years later with a similar although inverted fate* . . . *He who overcame death proves unable to live* (Lévi-Strauss 1960: 359)

Lévi-Strauss's own analysis is not the only Lévi-Straussian analysis that could be made of the myth.Some of his assumptions I find unconvincing. The girl's shyness at speaking her feelings need not be seen as a *natural* disability. Nor does anything in the text seem to justify Lévi-Strauss's contention that the youth is a "miraculous" hunter: he does not perform unusual hunting feats; he cannot even "pack animals very far," and he is never praised as an exceptional hunter. Hence the opposition between the girl and the youth in terms of their natural gifts seems overstated. Again, calling the fact that the orphan boy remains alone with his grand-mother a "social death" may be to impose a Western metaphor on Win-nebago thinking.

There are other parallelisms and oppositions in the myth which Lévi-Strauss has chosen not to dwell upon. The girl's indomitable love contrasts with the youth's lack of interest and with his immaturity (stressed by Radin in his notes). Both are strongly hampered in their movements: she as a ghost is unable to travel to ghost country. He is unable to hunt very far afield. Whereas in normal Winnebago life (and in the next myth we shall consider) the ghosts leave and the villagers stay, here the ghost stays and the villagers leave. Whereas normal hunters go after game, here the orphan boy expects game to come to him: "Animals might be driven in this direction . . . they might by chance come to this very timber and then I could occasionally kill some game" says he when refusing to follow the villagers.

The way the girl dies is both reversed and expanded in the trial the youth has to undergo in order to restore her to life. She could have recovered by saying but a word of her love; his telling stories for hours on end merely postpones his pains. She suffers because "continually, without abatement her mind kept invariably fixed on this;" he suffers because he cannot keep his mind on telling stories. She should have yielded to the compulsion to express her feelings; he must not yield to the compulsion to scratch himself.

The myth ends with the blessing the heroes become wolves bestow on fasting Indians. In terms of narrative consistency, this is unexpected. Yet in terms of underlying associations, it fits quite well: the two main episodes have to do with resistance to a compulsion – and what else is fasting? There is a progression from one type of compulsion to the next: the girl has no responsibility for her being in love. The youth is partly responsible for his compulsion to scratch, since he accepted the trial inflicted by the ghosts. The faster's hunger is directly self-inflicted. A morality is suggested: resistance to a compulsion should be proportionate with one's responsibility in it.

This interpretation differs from the one put forward by Lévi-Strauss, but there need not be any conflict. Many other interpretations could be suggested. This type of analysis aims at bringing out the symbolic *potential* of a myth rather than at ascribing to it a single structure once and for all. The claim underlying this approach is that complex outputs of "untamed" thinking, myths for instance, exhibit this kind of potential to a unique degree.

To some extent we can each make a different use of this potential, and it may be that the anthropologist's use of it never quite matches that of any native. However, the mythologist's aim is to give an account of the potential itself and not of the many ways in which it is individually exploited. Lévi-Strauss even adds (somewhat overstating the case):

If the final aim of anthropology is to contribute to a better knowledge of objectified thought and its mechanisms, it is in the last resort immaterial whether . . . the thought processes of the South American Indians take shape through the medium of my thought or whether mine take place through the medium of theirs (Lévi-Strauss 1969b: 13).

On anthropological knowledge

Showing that myths have a more complex internal structure than meets the ear is only the first part of Lévi-Strauss's program. The second part has to do with what may be called the "external structure" of a myth. Mythologists long ago established that there are strong resemblances to be found between different myths. Argument has raged as to whether these resemblances reflect common origins, identical stages in cultural evolution or universal categories of the human mind. Lévi-Strauss's contribution has been, first, to insist that resemblances are not the only close links to be found between myths. Similarity is one type of systematic relationship between them; inversion is another. Some myths are related to others in differing from them in a systematic way.

Further Lévi-Strauss argues that myths should not be analyzed one by one, but only as part of a group of related myths. Thus some aspects of the myth we have just discussed come out only when another Winnebago myth, the first in Radin's collection, is also taken into account. Here is my summary of this myth:[5]

A chief's son spent his time fasting in order "to acquire some powers from those various beings called the sacred ones . . . After a while he established a bond-friendship . . . devotedly he loved his friend." One day the chief's son was told that a war party was about to set out, but he was forbidden to tell anybody. He nevertheless told his friend and they both joined the warriors. The two friends fought with great bravery and were feasted by the villagers when they returned. They both became great warriors, married and went to live on their own lodges away from the village. Whenever they came into the village, "meticulous was the care bestowed upon them. Because of their accomplishments in war, the village had been greatly benefited by these two and they were honored and respected."

One day, they were about to set out on an expedition far afield for the sake of the villagers, but they were ambushed and, after much fighting, killed. Their ghosts returned to the village only to realize to their dismay that they had become invisible. Before setting out on their journey to the land of ghosts, they attended the Four Nights Wake celebrated for them. The chief's son's friend was so moved by the villagers' grief that he insisted they find a way to return. The chief's son said it could be done if they passed a test while on their journey.

They traveled and arrived at the first ghost village. They were extremely well received by beautiful men and women. A dance was held which lasted all night. However, the chief's son warned his friend: "Never get up to dance with them. If you get up, you will not attain your goal. This test was repeated for four nights and each night it proved more difficult.. Then the four nights of dancing were repeated in three other villages and each time it was more difficult not to join the dancers. They nevertheless succeeded and, in the end, could travel to the house of the Earthmaker. The Earthmaker gave them a choice of where to live again. They chose their own village and were reborn, each in his own family.

"And then, in the course of time they met each other and recognized each other although they were infants and although they were carried by others . . . They enjoyed this recognition very much . . . As they grew older they repeated what they had done in their previous existence."

80

What does this myth have to do with the earlier one? In both there is a death, a trial, and a resurrection, but there the parallel seems to end. The characters, circumstances, and mood of the two myths are otherwise quite different. On closer inspection, however, these seemingly random differences turn out to be systematic symmetries and oppositions.[6]

In the first myth, the heroes submit to their sad fate; in the second, they improve on their already glorious destiny. In the first, they are inordinately slow, the girl to speak, the boy to mature; he is unable to follow the villagers, she the ghosts. In the second myth, everything seems speeded up: the heroes become warriors before being of age; their moral and physical development is inordinately rapid; their mobility is extreme, they live away from the village, always ready to go on distant expeditions. Both myths have a cyclical character, but, in the first, the cycle goes from one generation to the next (the orphan boy eventually leaves behind him another orphan boy); whereas, in the the second, it is the same happy pair of heroes who start their lives all over again.

The relationships of symmetry and inversion between the two myths can be expressed in tabular form:

a chief's daughter	a chief's son
falls in love	makes a friend
she keeps silent when she should speak	he speaks when he should have kept silent
as a result of which she suffers and dies	as a result of which they fight and kill
the villagers leave the hero behind and go to live at a distance	the heroes leave the villagers behind and go to live at a distance
on one occasion the hero has to go further afield than usual to kill his quarry	on one occasion the two heroes are about to go further afield than usual and get killed
the hero comes back through the village and sees the ghost of the heroine	the heroes come back as ghosts to the village and cannot be seen
to bring the heroine back to life, the hero must undergo a four-night trial	to bring themselves back to life, the heroes must undergo four times a four-night trial
the trial consist in resisting the temptation to get rid of aggressive ghosts who have a repulsive non-human appearance	the trial consists in resisting the temptation to join friendly ghosts who have an attractive, quite human appearance
the hero succeeds, the heroine is resurrected, the villagers return	the heroes succeed and return to their village

81

the heroes give birth to a child	the heroes are born again as children
in spite of this resurrection the heroes cannot live. They become wolf-spirits, the protectors of fasters	thanks to this resurrection the heroes can live their lives again (and practice fasting)

Both myths display extraordinary character and events. Their heroes neither live nor die in the way ordinary people do. They achieve a kind of immortality, but in two different ways: the orphan boy and the chief's daughter by neither quite living nor quite dying; the warrior heroes by living and dying over and over again. These symmetrically opposed extraordinary fates provide points of reference for a Winnebago reflection on life and death.

In order to reach such an understanding, we have to examine several myths at a time. Then, and then only, many features become relevant, conceivable interpretations become more numerous and more precise. The anthropologist's task is to describe these virtualities, not to prescribe what uses should be made of them. The above analysis is not the only one that could be devised for the myths in question; if other myths were taken into account, other patterns of relationship would become apparent. Let us assume that the same is true of all myths, that they lend themselves better than other types of discourse to such analyzes. What theoretical implication would this have?

Lévi-Strauss is prone to claim that he has shown wonderful symmetries, perfect homologies or complete inversions in myths. Actually, there is more harmony in the descriptions than in the data. Perfect symmetries are achieved only by ignoring some of the data and by redescribing the rest in terms of carefully selected abstract synecdoches. But if we leave aside these exaggerations, there remains the exciting suspicion that the fleeting shapes and contours one can glimpse through the mist are those of true *terra incognita*. It is not belittling Lévi-Strauss's theoretical contribution to suggest that he may be first and foremost a discoverer of facts – the explorer of a mental continent which he is not to be reproached for having failed to chart fully.

Columbus thought he had reached the Indies. Lévi-Strauss often talks as if he had discovered a new language. Sometimes, however, he offers more promising suggestions. Discussions of myths often make use of linguistic metaphors. Taken literally, most of these metaphors are either meaningless or hopelessly paradoxical. If, for instance, the myths studied in *Mythologiques* belong to a single "language," then each American Indian society has access to only a small fragment of that language. Nobody (except possibly Lévi-Strauss himself) could be said to be even remotely fluent in it. What kind of a language is that?

As a structuralist, Lévi-Strauss should expect the analysis of a language to consist in identifying its minimal elements and then determining how these combine. He has indeed coined a term, "mytheme," for the minimal units of a myth, but thereafter has found little use for it. He has never put forward anything resembling a grammar of myths. Some of his pupils have tried to develop "linguistic" models, but he has paid no obvious attention to research he himself has inspired.

If myths were a language, then the question of their meaning would arise. Lévi-Strauss's approach to this question is first to organize the systems of correspondence underlying myths into separate "codes:" for instance, in the myths analyzed above, the heroes' travels and their changing locations could be said to pertain to a spatial code, and the social links involved – parenthood, marriage, chiefship, or friendship – to a social code. The relationships between elements within each code are then shown to correspond to those in other codes, and a complex pattern of such correspondences can be drawn up, displaying various levels of relationship: between elements, between codes, between episodes from the same myth, between myths, and so on. Lévi-Strauss calls these "meaning" relationships (notwithstanding the fact that they are reciprocal, whereas the relation of a signifier and a signified is not), and the system of such relationships a "matrix" of meanings:

Each matrix of meanings refers to another matrix, each myth to other myths. And if it is now asked to what final meaning these mutually significative meanings are referring – since in the last resort and in their totality they must refer to something – the only reply to emerge from this study is that myths signify the mind that evolves them by making use of the world of which it is itself a part (Lévi-Strauss 1969b: 340-341).

This cryptic statement may be clarified a little by another remark: "When the mind is left to commune with itself [as in myth, which 'has no obvious practical function'] and no longer has to come to terms with objects, it is in a sense reduced to imitating itself as object" (Lévi-Strauss 1969b: 10). One could argue, in the same vein, that in gymnastics the human body fulfills no obvious external function and is in a sense reduced to imitating itself. But this is a display rather than a coding. Similarly, assuming that fundamental mental mechanisms are displayed in myths, it does not follow that they are thereby *signified*.

Lévi-Strauss assumes *a priori* that myths convey symbolic meanings. Since these meanings are not apparent, he imagines them to be extraordinarily abstract. Yet, paradoxically, it can be claimed that one of Lévi-Strauss's greatest achievements in the treatment of myth (and of symbolism in general) is to have made it possible to dispense with the notion of meaning (see Sperber 1975a, Chapter 3). This is one achievement which Lévi-Strauss not only does not claim but implicitly *dis*claims, and this makes it particularly difficult to understand or assess his contribution to the study of myth.

The linguistic model is not the only one suggested by Lévi-Strauss. A myth, he maintains, is the transformation of other myths. This should be understood in two ways. A myth is a genetic transformation of other myths, in that myth-tellers never purely invent their stories, nor do they merely reproduce the stories they have heard (whether or not they are aware of the modifications they are bound to introduce in them). A myth is also a formal transformation of other myths in that, as we have seen, it can be "transformed" into any related myth by a number of more or less regular modifications, such as symmetrical inversion.

We have very little evidence on the actual genetic transformations which myths undergo. Ideally, one should follow several generations of myth-tellers, be present when they hear a myth, and present again when they retell it. What Lévi-Strauss's work suggests is that, although we cannot observe actual transformations in this way, we can try and reconstruct them speculatively: we can take formal transformations between related myths as hypothetical models for genetic transformations. This assumes that the modifications which myth-tellers are likely to make are not random departures from what they have heard but tend rather to consist in homologous replacements, symmetrical inversions, and so on. If this is the case, the regularities in the resulting myths could be accounted for by the actual process of their formation and transformation. It is as if oral transmission (with the demands it makes on memory and attention) selected over time regular forms in individual myths and regular relationships among myths belonging to the same culture. Viewed in this light, the facts brought out by Lévi-Strauss – all those odd correspondences and regularities – could possibly be accounted for as optimal properties for "untamed" thinking (more specifically, I would add, for storage and retrieval, in the absence of the external memory stores made available by writing). The study of myth could then throw light on little-known aspects of the human mind.

Lévi-Strauss achieved professional recognition through his work on kinship, and general recognition through his defense of structuralism. Yet it can be argued that, as his contribution to anthropology has developed, these two aspects have lost much of their central importance.

In its present impressive, yet incomplete, state, his work on kinship stands somewhat apart. *The Elementary Structures of Kinship* of 1949 was to have been followed by a further volume on "complex structures" which might have clarified the scope of Lévi-Strauss's theory of kinship and its significance for his view of the human mind.[7]

On the other hand, Lévi-Strauss seems to have exhausted all that he has to say on the subject of structuralism. His methodological writings have been fewer and fewer. The more recent ones merely defend or reformulate previously expressed ideas. There is no reason to doubt that structuralist methodology has played a major role in the elaboration of his views, but this is of historical rather than of theoretical relevance. From a theoretical point of view, Lévi-Strauss's structuralism is an odd mixture of sound principle and unsound expectations. It may have served a purpose, but by now it has become a hindrance to the full development of the very ideas that Lévi-Strauss contributed to anthropology.

Kinship

In conclusion to a review of *The Savage Mind*, Edmund Leach remarks:

Compared with cooking and music and the peculiarities of naming systems, the study of kinship and marriage is dull and pedestrian stuff, but for an anthropologist, kinship is the hard core, and for some of us Lévi-Strauss's retreat to the land of the Lotus-Eaters is, to some extent, a matter of regret (Leach 1967: 10)

I would argue that anthropologists have too often used the study of kinship as a retreat; as for its being dull and pedestrian stuff, one cannot but agree. Rather than go into technicalities, I shall point to links between Lévi-Strauss's work on kinship and his more general interests.

In all human societies there are rules about whom one can and whom one cannot marry. Some of these rules concern categories of relations, e.g., men may be forbidden to marry their "sisters" but allowed to marry their "cousins" ("sisters" and "cousins" are in inverted commas since here they stand for English native categories, not anthropological terms). Rather than merely forbidding or allowing, such rules may also take a more positive form: positive marriage rules state (more or less compellingly) that spouses should be chosen from among a given category, e.g., "a man should marry one of his "*nam*" (a Kachin native category for "matrilateral cross-cousins" in anthropological jargon).

For Lévi-Strauss, the condition which makes a kinship structure "elementary" is that it should include such a positive marriage rule. His approach to "elementary structures of kinship" was original in four main respects:

(a) He undertook to synthesize the available data on an unprecedented scale, and put forward a systematic classification of it. In his own words:

behind what seemed to be the superficial contingency and incoherent diversity of the laws governing marriage, I discerned a small number of simple principles, thanks to which a very complex mass of customs and practices, at first sight absurd (and generally held to be so), could be reduced to a meaningful system (Lévi-Strauss 1969b: 10).

This is an exaggeration in two respects: it is the elementary structures and not the laws governing marriage in general that are "reduced to a meaningful system;" furthermore, other anthropologists had already brought some order to the chaos. But despite these qualifications, Lévi-Strauss has advanced the systematic ordering of the data much further than any of his predecessors.

(b) Lévi-Strauss has developed the idea that, in elementary structures, the positive marriage rule is at the core of many institutions: relationships between descent groups, symbolic ordering of the society, cultural attitudes, etc. This is most clearly the case when the native categories used to refer to relatives also suggest the positive marriage rule. For instance, if the the term used for a man's mother's brother also denotes his wife's father, this suggests that a proper marriage is one that takes place with the mother's brother's daughter. When all in-laws are consistently called by terms used for kin – that is to say when there is no terminological distinction between kin and affines – both the way in which relationships work and the way in which people conceive of them are bound to be affected. One of the most novel and valuable aspects of Lévi-Strauss's work has been to pay systematic attention to the close connection between positive marriage rules and these peculiar terminologies, and to show how, together, they are central to a whole set of institutions and cultural representations.

(c) A third source of originality in Lévi-Strauss's approach was his attempt to account for kinship structures in terms of basic mental structures:

What are the mental structures to which we have referred and the universality of which can be established? It seems there are three: the exigency of the rule as a rule; the notion of reciprocity regarded as the most immediate form of integrating the opposition between the self and others; and finally the synthetic nature of the gift, i.e., that the agreed transfer of a valuable from one individual to another makes these individuals into partners, and adds a new quality to the valuable transferred (Lévi-Strauss 1969b: 84)

Lévi-Strauss's systematic classification of positive marriage rules is based on the "principle of reciprocity." His integration of various aspects of kinship around the marriage rule is largely related to the "synthetic nature of the gift." But it could not be claimed that he has done more in this connection than show a certain congruence between specific social forms and some very general principles (which pertain to the philosophy of law rather than to psychology). The psychological import of his conclusions is unclear and, conversely, psychological considerations have little bearing on them. Lévi-Strauss has himself explained why it should be so.

In *Elementary Structures of Kinship*, he says, "there was nothing to guarantee that the obligations came from within. Perhaps they were merely the reflections in men's minds of certain social demands that had been objectified in institutions" (Lévi-Strauss 1969b: 10). He then goes on to argue, quite soundly, that the study of myths should be much more directly relevant to the understanding of the human mind.

(d) A fourth source of originality in Lévi-Strauss's approach is implied in the title of his book, *The Elementary Structures of Kinship*. He holds that marriage systems based on a positive rule are *elementary*; their study should serve as the basis for a general theory of kinship. These systems are elementary in that the principles on which they explicitly organize the "circulation of women" are at work in all societies. In complex structures, these principles are implicit and lost to view among many other factors.

Strong doubts have been expressed about the possibility of generalizing from "elementary structures" to kinship in general, most notably by the British anthropologists Edmund Leach (1970) and Rodney Needham (1971). Needham in particular, backed by a long tradition, calls "prescriptive" the systems where terminology and marriage rule coincide, and "preferential" the systems where the positive rule is not already implied in the terminology. He argues that only in "prescriptive" systems has there been shown to exist a true systematic integration of social institutions and symbolic representations around the marriage rule. He questions the very idea that "kinship structures" are to be found in every society.

Lévi-Strauss mistook Needham's technical distinction between "prescriptive" and "preferential" for an ordinary language, one synonymous with that between "obligatory" and "optional." On this wrong premise, Lévi-Strauss argues quite correctly, but irrelevantly, that in no society is the marriage rule followed without exceptions; thus, rather than two types, there is a continuum of cases of more or less stringent rules. But of course Needham's distinction has to do with the type of terminology, and not with the stringency of the rule. Beyond this misunderstanding, one substantial issue is involved: is the integration of kinship into a system built around a marriage rule present in all societies? Or does this kind of system only exist in some societies, those with "prescriptive alliance?"

Lévi-Strauss seems to resent the suggestion that his approach might be directly relevant to "prescriptive" systems only. If this were so, he writes,

I would have written a very fat book which since 1952 has aroused all sorts of commentaries and discussions despite its being concerned with such rare facts and so limited a field that it is difficult to understand of what interest it would be with regard to a general theory of kinship (Lévi-Strauss 1969a: xxxi).

Still, as long as the study of "complex structures" has not satisfactorily established that "elementary structures" are truly elementary, the onus of the proof is on Lévi-Strauss. Skepticism in the matter implies no disparagement. There are several hundred known "prescriptive" systems. A study throwing light on these systems is of an unusually large scope: after all, most anthropologists spend their life studying just one or two societies.

Polemics aside, what is the issue? A comparison may help clarify it. In all societies, people age and generations follow one another. Some societies, in the Horn of Africa for instance,[8] have evolved elaborate systems of age sets and generation grades which play a crucial integrating role. A Lévi-Straussian approach might consist in showing that these greatly varied systems are based on a few fundamental principles. These principles could then serve as as a basis for classification and help explain the importance of these institutions. One might be tempted, at this stage, to suggest that age sets and generation grades are the "elementary structures of generationality," and to assume that all societies have a generational system, whether "elementary" or "complex." Most anthropologists would object that the many aspects and stages of age and generational transition come under a variety of different institutions and are not integrated in one structure.

Now, it could be argued that so-called "elementary structures of kinship," with their elaborate rules and institutions, are similar to generation grades: they integrate in a single structure aspects of social life which, in other societies, come under various institutions. Even so, the principles put forward in the study of positive marriage rules may be of general relevance. For instance Lévi-Strauss's elaboration of the "principle of reciprocity" has inspired further research on economic and ritual systems.

Whether "elementary structures of kinship" are truly elementary or not is still an open question (if it is a well posed question at all). More generally, it is difficult to place Lévi-Strauss's monumental study of kinship within work which, since then, has turned directly to the anthropological study of the human mind. Why this difficulty? Possibly because, in *The Elementary Structures*, two views of anthropology meet and clash as much as they complement one another. The questions asked still belong to an anthropology in the service of ethnography, an anthropology whose tasks are to put some order into the data of ethnographers and to provide them with interpretive tools. The solutions put forward already belong to a truly anthropological anthropology, i.e., a study of cultural variation aimed at a better understanding of universal mental structures.

Structuralism

The word "structuralism" has suffered from its popularity. It has been used in many different senses and sometimes with no sense at all. In the heat of the 1968 "May events" in France, a leading French football coach sternly declared that time had come to "revise the structuralism" of the national team. Given this variety of application, I shall limit myself to Lévi-Strauss's own uses of the term and not inquire whether – or how – they connect up with its other uses. There is however one connection which Lévi-Strauss himself stresses: that with structuralist linguistics in the tradition of Saussure.

Three principles of this tradition have been particularly relevant to the development of Lévi-Strauss's views. Firstly, language should be studied in itself, and only after that may its relationships to other systems, historical, sociological, or psychological, be considered: internal structure takes precedence over external function. Secondly, speech, the perceptible manifestation of language, is to be broken down into a finite number of minimal elements, such as phonemes on the phonological level. Thirdly, the elements of a language are to be defined by their mutual relationships. These relationships are of two kinds: paradigmatic relationships between elements that can be substituted for one another; syntagmatic relationships between elements which can combine together. Lévi-Strauss has adapted these three principles to his own anthropological ends.

When generalized, the first principle states that a proper object for scientific investigation must be a set of facts having internal coherence and external autonomy. Selecting such an object is a crucial first step. Lévi-Strauss's criticism of earlier views on totemism is precisely this: that the set of facts which had been brought together did not have the required coherence and autonomy.

Of this first principle, Lévi-Strauss can quite rightly claim that it is part of scientific method in general. By stressing it, he has helped to introduce a greater concern for methodological soundness among anthropologists. At the same time, since the principle can hardly be controverted, it does not distinguish structuralist methodology from scientific methodology in general. If, as Lévi-Strauss sometimes seems to be claiming, structuralism means nothing more than a scientific approach, we should drop the term and go back to "scientific," to avoid football coaches and some others becoming utterly confused.

The search for minimal elements, although Lévi-Strauss claims it is an essential step in anthropology also, plays only a minor role in his actual investigations. As we have seen, he coined a term, "mytheme," for the minimal units of a myth, and then failed to make use of it. He also asserted the existence of "atoms of kinship," and built interesting hypotheses around them. However, these "atoms," unlike phonemes or morphemes in structural linguistics, are neither minimal nor elementary units. Anyhow, not everything in the world can be analyzed into a finite set of "minimal elements." There are continuous functions, infinite and non-enumerable sets, and classes which can be defined only intensionally an not extensionally. There are also many cases – and judging from Lévi-Strauss's actual practice, myth is one of them – where to look for minimal elements is not the best approach. The structuralist expectation that any coherent and autonomous domain can be usefully characterized in terms of a finite set of minimal elements is unwarranted.

The third principle is that a proper structural description should be a characterization of paradigmatic and syntagmatic relationships. When elements can be isolated, it is generally quite easy to order them in such a way. But in most cases (language being one of them if we accept Chomsky's critique of structuralist linguistics) such an ordering is of no great use – and why should it be? Here again is a principle which Lévi-Strauss has occasionally illustrated, but never properly followed.

To those three principles carried over from linguistics into anthropology, Lévi-Strauss has added a fourth: he claims that related structures are transformations of one another, and that the rules governing these transformations constitute a more abstract and general level of analysis. The notion of "transformation" can be understood in a very weak sense, such that anything can be said to stand in a relationship of transformation with anything else. With "transformation" so weakly understood, Lévi-Strauss's fourth principle would be vacuous. With any stronger notion of transformation, on the other hand, this principle seems quite arbitrary. Still, two cases, those of mythical transformations and of mathematical models of kinship, could be claimed to illustrate this principle. In each of these cases, however, "transformation" is specified quite differently.

It might well be asked why Lévi-Strauss should have bothered to put forward a "structuralist" method based on principles which he himself does not feel impelled to follow. I can see two reasons for this. In the 1940s and '50s, many scholars set great store by the development of a unified science of communication integrating semiotics, cybernetics, and information theory. This science would bring together the study of language, culture, and society with that of the human brain and mind. Common concepts, and a common method, would lead to a new scientific take-off. Lévi-Strauss's early methodological papers were meant as contributions to this new science. He probably expected that they would soon be superseded by further advances along the same lines, made by him or by others.

Thirty years later, it has become clear that such expectations were largely unjustified. The important advances that have taken place in these particular fields owe little or nothing, except a jargon, to any unified science of communication. Because Lévi-Strauss has devoted himself to the furtherance of his own discipline, he has, in practice, left his earlier methodological optimism on one side. But hopes are not easily given up. He may believe that his expectations will still prove to have been justified and that there is no compelling reason why he should reconsider principles which have never yet been properly exploited.

Lévi-Strauss's structuralist stance must also be understood in the context of the rationalist/empiricist controversy. In asserting that cultures have developed not simply in response to external demands but, more fundamentally, in accordance with the human mind's internal constraints, Lévi-Strauss took a major step away from strict empiricism. He did it at a time when empiricism exercised an almost total domination over the social and psychological sciences, under such labels as "behaviorism" in psychology and "cultural relativism" in anthropology. As a result he came under constant attack. Understandably, he chose to defend his first having taken this step rather than advancing further in the rationalist direction in which it was leading him. The very simple and homogeneous structures which structuralism postulates served to make this reintroduction of the human mind into anthropology much more acceptable. The structuralist mind is as tidy as crystal; it has no room for odd-looking or specialized "innate devices."

With the passage of time, one thing has become clear: if the human mind is a proper subject of study – and why shouldn't it be? – there is no sense in laying down what kind or degree of structure one ought to find in it. It is hard to comprehend now why it was once thought that the brain must have a simpler structure than, say, the hand. The only way to follow up Lévi-Strauss's initial step towards a better understanding of the workings of the human mind is to eliminate any *a priori* limitations on what one is permitted to find. In this respect, structuralism allows, paradoxically, for too little by way of structure.

There is one other important way in which Lévi-Strauss uses the word "structuralism," and that is to refer to any general aspect of his own work. For instance, he would say that it was "structuralist" to pay attention in myths as much to their systematic differences as to resemblances, or to refuse to be satisfied with a description of "totemism" which accounts only for its form and not for its content. Such an approach derives less from any original principles than from an intellectual attitude both bold and demanding. Together with his many profound insights, it is this attitude which has enabled Lévi-Strauss to make a truly general and also very personal contribution to anthropology in its widest sense. That he should attribute his own individual creativeness to an abstract "structuralism" is modesty on his part. To follow him in this would be to show either submissiveness or ingratitude.

By its monumental character, the work of Lévi-Strauss evokes that of the founders of modern anthropology, from Morgan to Frazer. By the manner in which it relates the cultural and the mental, it may anticipate a theoretical anthropology yet to come. In contemporary anthropology, however, it is alone of its kind. In spite of this singularity, Lévi-Strauss's work is, more than any other, symptomatic of the current predicament of anthropology.

Today, there is no general "anthropological theory" more elaborate than Lévi-Strauss's. However, as he would himself agree, his hypotheses are not "scientific" as the word is understood in physics or in biology. They lack the univocity and the precision needed for proper empirical testing. They allow, on the contrary, some scope for interpretation, depending on the context and the reader. Lévi-Strauss himself interprets and reinterprets his own words and does not attempt to separate hypotheses from exegeses, or corollaries from commentaries. Yet, like most contemporary anthropologists, he keeps invoking the scientific ideal.

In order to be scientific, an hypothesis must be general, non-trivial and rigorous enough to be testable. Often, out of these three conditions, only rigor is remembered; rigor is identified with science, and taken for an end in itself when, in fact, it is only a means towards an end: making an hypothesis empirically testable. The social sciences are full of general truisms and of minute observations presented with finicky rigor, but no bold generalization ever grows on such dry soil. Few are the scholars who, since choose they must, give precedence to theoretical imagination, hoping, rightly or wrongly, that rigor will follow. Few are those who can afford such a choice. Lévi-Strauss is one of them, even though all his writings, with their methodological proclamations and their rhetorical formalism, evince a longing for a rigor still out of reach.

No truly rigorous hypotheses, no plain factual evidence either. Lévi-Strauss cannot but use the data of ethnography, which consist not in observations but in interpretations, or even in interpretations of interpretations. He himself presents these data only after having reinterpreted them to suit his purpose. Thus, in his anthropological writings, we find not mythical narratives, but summaries of translations of these narratives, not native words revealing underlying "beliefs," but chosen excerpts of the "world-views" distilled by ethnographers from the words of their hosts, not observations of rituals, but fragments of ritual scenarios reconstructed by ethnographers on the basis of what they have heard and seen. None of this is peculiar to Lévi-Strauss: the same situation prevails throughout anthropology and in most social sciences. In such conditions, even if we had truly scientific hypotheses, we might well lack a way to test them empirically.

In his presentation of evidence or in his most abstract speculations, Lévi-Strauss appeals to the intuitive assent of his readers more than to their reasoning abilities: to convince, he captivates. If, in this respect, he differs from other anthropologists, it is in showing greater virtuosity, but his discourse is of the same type as theirs.

Claude Lévi-Strauss today

Anthropological and ethnographic discourse proceeds between observation and theory without ever quite pertaining to the one or the other. It is an interpretive discourse: it is not about things, but about the anthropologist's understanding of things. It is an account of an intuitive experience, the ethnographer's individual experience of the collective experience of his hosts. The anthropologist may move away from this concrete level of experience without thereby getting any closer to the level of theory. A good part of anthropological abstraction is mere abstraction: as in painting, you may like it or not, but it does not represent anything.

Only exceptionally does anthropological discourse move from an a-theoretical to pre-theoretical level, that is to general hypotheses which are neither trivial nor absurd, and the empirical import of which is not wholly indiscernible. Lévi-Strauss reaches this pre-theoretical level when he goes beyond making intuitively perceptible properties of cultural phenomena, and considers the psychological foundations of these intuitions. Intuition, which is an instrument of ethnography, becomes an object of study for anthropology.

Notes

Introduction

1. There are useful comments on Protagoras's fable (reported by Plato – see Taylor's translation 1976) and on the ideas of the Sophist in Baldry 1965, Bodin 1975, Dupréel 1948, Guthrie 1969, Untersteiner 1954, Vernant 1955. Most comments, however, dwell on the distinction between the gifts of Prometheus and those of Hermes and pay little attention to the way in which Protagoras contrasts humans with other animals. This might be due to the fact that (leaving aside mythological flourish) modern conceptions of that contrast are not very different from Protagoras's.
2. This text has recently been republished and discussed by Moore 1969, Moravia 1970, Copans & Jamin 1978. See also Jorion 1980.
3. "Cultural anthropology" and "social anthropology" have meanings which are too similar and too vague to be worth distinguishing. They both refer to the study of socio-cultural phenomena, be it general, comparative, or local. One should just note the preference of British anthropologists, who used to favor a more sociological approach, for the epithet "social," and that of American anthropologists, who used to show greater interest for psychology, for the epithet "cultural." "Ethnography" is generally used – and will be used here – in a more restricted sense: it refers exclusively to the study of socio-cultural phenomena *within* a specific human group.
4. Beside Malinowski's own writings, see Firth 1957, and Panoff 1972.

1. Interpretive ethnography and theoretical anthropology

1. See Radcliffe-Brown 1952, and 1957, in particular pp. 146-148.
2. See Geertz 1973, 1983; see also Ricoeur 1971, Rabinow and Sullivan 1979
3. See Agar 1980 for a development and an illustration of this argument.
4. See McHale 1978. To the strictly grammatical notion of free indirect speech, one might prefer a logical notion such as that of implicit mention of propositions, but I shan't go into that here (see Sperber & Wilson 1981).
5. A mistake I committed in the first published version of this paper (Sperber 1981).
6. Favret-Saada 1980 is, in this respect, a remarkable exception; see also Levy 1973.
7. See Leach 1961, Needham 1971, 1972, and 1975. The following considerations owe much to Needham.

8. See Robertson Smith 1889, Hubert & Mauss 1964, Leach 1976.
9. See for instance Bateson 1972, Barth 1975, Goodenough 1981.
10. Lévi-Strauss 1969b, 1971, 1973c, 1978. For a comparison with Dumézil's seminal ideas, see Smith & Sperber 1971.
11. See Cavalli-Sforza & Feldman 1981, Lumsden & Wilson 1981, and also Dawkins 1976.
12. A point stressed by Lumsden and Wilson 1981. This makes their work less inadequate, regarding human cultures, than the earlier works of Wilson (1975, 1978) which caused heavy polemics (see in particular Sahlins 1977).
13. Johnson-Laird and Wason 1977 is a representative collection of papers, though already somewhat outdated. Two journals, *Cognition* and *Brain and Behavior Science* are particularly worth following. Chomsky 1980, Dennett 1978, Dreske 1981, and Fodor 1975, 1981, 1983 discuss central issues of the field.
14. See however Cole & Scribner 1974, Rosch & Lloyd 1978, Hutchins 1980.
15. I suggested elements of an answer in Sperber 1975a, 1980.
16. For instance Keil 1979, Macnamara 1982, Miller & Johnson-Laird 1976, Rosch & Lloyd 1978, Smith & Medin 1981; Mandler & Johnson 1977, Rumelhardt 1975, Thorndyke 1977, Zan; Lakoff & Johnson 1980, Ortony 1979.
17. See Berlin & Kay 1969, Tornay 1978.

2. Apparently irrational beliefs

1. Among recent discussions, see Wilson (ed.) 1970, Finnegan & Horton (eds.) 1973, Gellner 1975, Skorupski 1976, Hookway & Pettit (eds.) 1978, Lukes & Hollis (eds.) 1982. Quine 1960 is in the background of most of the discussions.
2. Another line of argument for relativism is based on philosophical skepticism (e.g., Quine 1960). It is irrelevant, however, to the assessment of relativism as a theory in the empirical sciences, and hence to my present perspective.
3. It has been discussed by Durkheim & Mauss 1963, Lévy-Bruhl 1911, Cassirer 1955, Vygotsky 1962, Geertz 1973, among others.
4. It has been suggested that even logical rules might be culture-specific, but no one has ever worked out what this might involve empirically.
5. The following discussion is in part inspired by Chomsky 1975, 1980, and Fodor 1975. See also Sperber 1974.
6. See for instance Cole & Scribner 1974, Triandis et al. 1980.
7. For a discussion of Berlin & Kay's work from a relativist point of view, see Sahlins 1976.
8. For examples of recent discussions, see Bobrow & Collins (eds.) 1975, Cofer (ed.) 1976, Loftus & Loftus 1976.
9. For a recent statement of this commonly held view, see Pouillon 1979.
10. Note that saying that there are semi-propositional representations does not commit one to the existence of "semi-propositions" (just as saying that there are incomplete addresses does not commit one to the existence of "semi-domiciles").
11. A comparable though not identical distinction has been suggested by de Souza 1971, and developed by Dennett 1978, CH. 16. See also Skorupski 1978.
12. See once more Favret-Saada 1980 for a remarkable exception.

13. Of course, if your sole aim is knowledge and if you want not just to achieve, but to maximize rationality, you should not trust easily and you should be weary of semi-propositional representations with no proper interpretation in sight, but doing so might be at the expense of rationality in social relations.
14. "Je sais bien, mais quand même . . . ," the basic formula of believers argued the psychoanalyst O. Mannoni in a now classic paper (Mannoni 1969, ch. 1).

3. Claude Lévi-Strauss today

1. Lévi-Strauss writes of structural thinking: "only those who practice it know, through intimate experience, this sense of fulfilment that its exercise provides, and through which the mind feels that it truly communes with the body" (1971: 619).
2. A point suggested to me by Jean-Pierre Vernant.
3. Notwithstanding some interesting but limited resemblances with Dumézil's approach. See Smith and Sperber 1971.
4. Addressing readers of the original text, Lévi-Strauss merely evokes the content of the myth. In the following summary, passages within inverted commas are quoted from Radin 1949:77–95.
5. Passages within quotation marks are quoted from Radin 1949:12–36.
6. The following analysis is inspired by, but not identical with Lévi-Strauss's own.
7. Lévi-Strauss has recently taken up again the question of "complex structures." There may be, therefore, a follow up to *The Elementary Structures*. See also Héritier 1981.
8. See Legesse 1973, Baxter & Almagor 1978.

References

Agar, Michael (1980). "Hermeneutics in anthropology." *Ethos* 8 (3). 253-272.
Baldry, H.C. (1965). *The Unity of Mankind in Greek Thought*. Cambridge: Cambridge University Press.
Barth, Fredrik (1975). *Ritual and Knowledge among the Baktaman of New Guinea*. New Haven: Yale University Press.
Bateson, Gregory (1972). *Steps to an Ecology of the Mind*. New York: Ballantine Books.
Bauman, Richard & Joel Sherzer (eds.) (1974). *Explorations in the Ethnography of Speaking*. Cambridge: Cambridge University Press.
Baxter, P.T.W. & Uri Almagor (eds.) (1978). *Age, Generation and Time*. London: Hurst and Co.
Berlin, Brent (1978). "Ethnobiological Classification." Eleanor Rosch & Barbara Lloyd (eds.).*Cognition and Categorization*. Hillsdale: Lawrence Erlbaum. 9-26.
Berlin, Brent & Paul Kay (1969). *Basic Color Terms: Their Universality and Evolution*. Berkeley: University of California Press.
Bloch, Maurice (ed.) (1975) *Political Language and Oratory in Traditional Society*. London: Academic Press.
Bobrow, D.G. & Allan Collins (eds.) (1975). *Representation and Understanding: Studies in Cognitive Science* New York: Academic Press.
Bodin, Louis (1975). *Lire le Protagoras*. Paris: Les Belles Lettres.
Cassirer, Ernst (1955). *The Philosophy of Symbolic Forms, Volume Two: Mythical Thought*. Translated by R. Manheim. New Haven: Yale University Press.
Cavalli-Sforza L.L. & M.W. Feldman (1981). *Cultural Transmission and Evolution: A Quantitative Approach*. Princeton: Princeton University Press.
Chomsky, Noam (1975). *Reflections on Language*. New York: Pantheon.
(1980). *Rules and Representations*. New York: Columbia University Press.
Cofer, Charles N. (ed.) (1976) *The Structure of Human Memory*. San Francisco: Freeman.
Cole, Michael & Sylvia Scribner (1974). *Culture and Thought: A Psychological Introduction*. New York: Wiley.
Copans, Jean & Jean Jamin (1978). *Aux Origines de l'Anthropologie Française: Les Mémoires de la Société des Observateurs de l'Homme*. Paris: Le Sycomore.
Crocker, J.C. (1977). "My Brother the Parrot." In J. David Sapir & J.C. Crocker (eds.) *The Social Use of Metaphor*. Philadelphia: University of Pennsylvania Press. 164-192.

References

Dawkins, R. (1976). *The Selfish Gene*. Oxford; Oxford University Press.
Degérando, J.-M. (1969). *The Observation of Savage Peoples*. Translated by F.C.T. Moore. London: Routledge and Kegan Paul.
Dennett, Daniel C. (1978). *Brainstorms: Philosophical Essays on Mind and Psychology*. Hassocks: Harvester Press.
Douglas, Mary (1966). *Purity and Danger: An Analysis of the Concepts of Pollution and Taboo*. London: Routledge and Kegan Paul.
—— (1975). *Implicit Meanings: Essays in Anthropology*. London: Routledge and Kegan Paul.
Dreske, Fred I. (1981). *Knowledge and the Flow of Information*. Cambridge, Mass.: The M.I.T. Press.
Dupréel, Eugène (1948). *Les Sophistes*. Neûchatel: Editions du Griffon.
Durkheim, Emile & Marcel Mauss (1963). *Primitive Classification*. Translated by R. Needham. Chicago: University of Chicago Press.
Evans-Pritchard, E.E. (1956). *Nuer Religion*. Oxford: Clarendon Press.
—— (1962). *Essays in Social Anthropology*. London: Faber.
Favret-Saada, Jeanne (1980). *Deadly Words*. Translated by C. Cullen. Cambridge: Cambridge University Press.
Finnegan, Ruth & Robin Horton (eds.) (1973). *Modes of Thought*. London: Faber.
Firth, Raymond (ed.) (1957). *Man and Culture: An Evaluation of the Work of Bronislaw Malinowski*. London: Routledge and Kegan Paul.
Fodor, Jerry (1975). *The Language of Thought*. New York: Crowell.
—— (1981). *Representations*. Cambridge, Mass.: M.I.T. Press.
—— (1983). *The Modularity of Mind* Cambridge, Mass.: M.I.T. Press.
Geertz, Clifford (1966). "Religion as a Cultural System." In Michael Banton (ed.) *Anthropological Approaches to the Study of Religion*. London: Tavistock. 1-46. Reprinted in Geertz 1973: 87-125.
—— (1973). *The Interpretation of Cultures: Selected Essays*. New York: Basic Books.
—— (1983). *Local Knowledge: Further Essays in Interpretive Anthropology*. New York: Basic Books.
Gellner, Ernest (1975). *The Legitimation of Belief*. Cambridge: Cambridge University Press.
Goodenough, Ward H. *Culture, Language and Society*, second edition (first edition 1971). Menlo Park: The Benjamin Cummings Publication Company.
Goody, Jack (1977). *The Domestication of the Savage Mind*. Cambridge: Cambridge University Press.
Griaule, Marcel (1948). *Dieu d'Eau*. Paris: Editions du Chêne.
Guidieri, Remo (1980). *La Route des Morts*. Paris: Le Seuil.
Guthrie, W.K.C. (1969). *A History of Greek Philosophy, Volume III: The Fifth Century Enlightenment*. Cambridge: Cambridge University Press.
Harman, Gilbert (1973). *Thought*. Princeton: Princeton University Press.
Héritier, Françoise (1981). *L'Exercice de la Parenté*. Paris: Gallimard/Le Seuil.
Hookway, C. & Philip Pettit (eds.) (1978). *Action and Interpretation: Studies in the Philosophy of the Social Sciences*. Cambridge: Cambridge University Press.
Horton, Robin (1961). "Destiny and the Unconscious in West Africa." *Africa* 23 (2). 110-116.
—— (1967). "African Traditional Thought and Western Science." *Africa* 37 (1)

References

50-71 and (2) 155-187. Reprinted in Brian Wilson (ed.). *Rationality*. Oxford: Blackwell. 131-171.

Hubert, H & Marcel Mauss.(1964). *Sacrifice: Its Nature and Function*. Translated by W.D. Halls. London: Cohen and West.

Hutchins, Edwin (1980). *Culture and Inference: A Trobriand Case Study*. Cambridge, Mass.: Harvard University Press.

Izard, Michel & Pierre Smith (1979). *La Fonction Symbolique: Essais d'Anthropologie*. Paris: Gallimard.

Johnson-Laird, P.N. & P.C. Wason (eds.) (1977). *Thinking: Readings in Cognitive Science*. Cambridge: Cambridge University Press.

Jorion, Paul (1980). "Aux Origines de l'Anthropologie Française." *L'Homme*, 20 (2) 91-98.

Keil, Frank C. (1979). *Semantic and Conceptual Development: An Ontological Perspective* Cambridge, Mass.: Harvard University Press.

Lakoff, George & Mark Johnson (1980). *Metaphors We Live By*. Chicago: University of Chicago Press.

Leach, Edmund (1961). *Rethinking Anthropology*. London: Athlone Press.

(1967). "Brain Twister." *New York Review of Books*, 12 October, 6-10.

(1970). *Lévi-Strauss*. London: Fontana.

(1976). *Culture and Communication*. Cambridge: Cambridge University Press.

Legesse, Asmarom (1973). *Gada: Three Approaches to the Study of African Society*. Glencoe: Free Press.

Lévi-Strauss, Claude (1960). "Four Winnebago Myths. A Structural Sketch." In Stanley Diamond (ed.) *Culture and History*. New York: Columbia University Press. 351-362.

(1963a). *Structural Anthropology*. Translated by C.Jacobson & B. G. Schoepf. New York: Basic Books.

(1963b). *Totemism*. Translated by R. Needham. Boston: Beacon Press.

(1966). *The Savage Mind*. London: Weidenfeld & Nicolson.

(1969a). *The Elementary Structures of Kinship*. Translated by J.H. Bell, J.R. von Sturmer & R. Needham (ed.). Boston: Beacon Press.

(1969b). *The Raw and the Cooked*. Translated by J. & D. Weightman. London: Jonathan Cape.

(1971). *L'Homme Nu*. Paris: Plon.

(1973a). *Anthropologie Structurale Deux*. Paris: Plon.

(1973b). *Tristes Tropiques*. Translated by J. & D. Weightman. London: Jonathan Cape.

(1973c). *From Honey to Ashes*. Translated by J. & D. Weightman. London: Jonathan Cape.

(1975). *La Voie des Masques*. Genève: Skira.

(1978). *The Origin of Table Manners*. Translated by J. & D. Weightman. London: Jonathan Cape.

Levy, R.I. (1973). *Tahitians*. Chicago: University of Chicago Press.

Lévy-Bruhl, Lucien (1911). *Les Fonctions Mentales Dans les Sociétés Inférieures*. Paris: Alcan.

Lienhardt, Godfrey (1954). "The Shilluk of the Upper Nile." In D.Forde (ed.). *African Worlds*. Oxford: Oxford University Press. 138-163.

Loftus, Elisabeth & Geoffrey Loftus (1976). *Human Memory*. Hillsdale: Lawrence Erlbaum.

Lukes, Steven (1967). "Some Problems about Rationality." *Archives Eur-*

References

opéennes de Sociologie, 8. 247-264. Reprinted in B. Wilson (ed.) *Rationality*. Oxford: Blackwell.

Lukes, Steven & Martin Hollis (eds.) (1982). *Rationality and Relativism*. Oxford: Blackwell.

Lumsden, C.J. & Edward O. Wilson (1981). *Genes, Mind and Culture*. Cambridge, Mass.: Harvard University Press.

Lydall, Jean & Ivo Stecker (1979). *The Hamar of Southern Ethiopia, vol. II: Baldambe Explains*. Hohenschaftlarn: Klaus Renner.

McHale, B. (1978). "Free Indirect Discourse: A Survey of Recent Accounts." *PTL: A Journal for Descriptive Poetics and the Theory of Literature*, 3. 249-287.

Macnamara, John (1982). *Names for Things*. Cambridge, Mass.: M.I.T. Press.

Malinowski, Bronislaw (1922). *Argonauts of the Western Pacific*. London: Routledge.

(1967). *A Diary in the Strict Sense of the Term*. London: Routledge and Kegan Paul.

Mandler, Jean M. & N.S. Johnson (1977). "Remembrance of Things Parsed: Story Structure and Recall." *Cognitive Psychology*, 9. 111-151.

Mannoni, O. (1969). *Clefs pour l'Imaginaire ou l'Autre Scène*. Paris: Le Seuil.

Miller, George A. & P. Johnson-Laird (1976). *Language and Perception*. Cambridge: Cambridge University Press.

Moore, F.C.T. (1969). "Translator's Introduction." In J.-M. Degérando, *The Observation of Savage Peoples*. London: Routledge and Kegan Paul.

Moravia, Sergio (1970). *La Scienza dell'Uomo nel Settecento*. Bari: Laterza.

Needham, Rodney (ed.) (1971). *Rethinking Kinship and Marriage*. London: Tavistock.

Needham, Rodney (1972). *Belief Language and Experience*. Oxford: Blackwell.

(1975). "Polythetic Classification." *Man*, 10. 349-369.

Ortony, Andrew (ed.) (1979). *Metaphor and Thought*. Cambridge: Cambridge University Press.

Panoff, Michel (1972). *Bronislaw Malinowski*. Paris: Payot.

Plato (1976). *Protagoras*. Translated with notes by C.C. Taylor. Oxford: Clarendon Press.

Pouillon, J. (1979). "Remarques sur le Verbe Croire." In Michel Izard & Pierre Smith (eds.), *La Fonction Symbolique: Essais d'Anthropologie*. Paris: Gallimard.

Quine, Willard van Orman (1960). *Word and Object* Cambridge, Mass.: M.I.T. Press.

Rabinow, Paul & William M. Sullivan (eds.) (1979). *Interpretive Social Science*. Berkeley: University of California Press.

Radcliffe-Brown, A.R. (1952). *Structure and Function in Primitive Society*. London: Cohen and West.

(1957). *A Natural Science of Society*. Glencoe: Free Press.

Radin, Paul (1949). *The Culture of the Winnebago: As Described by Themselves*. Memoir of the *International Journal of American Linguistics*.

Ricoeur, Paul (1971). "The Model of the Text: Meaningful Action Considered as Text." *Social Research*, 38. Reprinted in Paul Rabinow & William M. Sullivan (eds.) (1979). *Interpretive Social Science*. Berkeley: University of California Press.

Rosch, Eleanor (1974). "Linguistic Relativity." In A. Silverstein (ed.). *Human Communication: Theoretical Perspective*. Hillsdale: Lawrence Erlbaum.

102

References

Rosch, Eleanor & Barbara Lloyd (eds.) (1978).*Cognition and Categorization.* Hillsdale: Lawrence Erlbaum.

Rumelhardt, David E. (1975). "Notes on a Schema for Stories." In D.G. Bobrow, & Allan Collins (eds.). *Representation and Understanding: Studies in Cognitive Science* New York: Academic Press.

Sahlins, Marshall (1976). "Colors and Cultures." *Semiotica*, 16. 1-22.

(1977). *The Use and Abuse of Biology.* Ann Arbor: The University of Michigan Press.

Skorupski, John (1976). *Symbol and Theory: A Philosophical Study of Theories of Religion in Social Anthropology.* Cambridge: Cambridge University Press.

(1978). "The Meaning of Another Culture's Beliefs." In C. Hookway & Philip Pettit (eds.) *Action and Interpretation: Studies in the Philosophy of the Social Sciences.* Cambridge: Cambridge University Press. 83-106.

Smith, Edward E. & D.L. Medin (1981). *Categories and Concepts.* Cambridge, Mass.: Harvard University Press.

Smith, Pierre & Dan Sperber (1972). "Mythologiques de Georges Dumézil." *Annales* 26. 559-586.

Smith, Robertson (1889). *Lectures on the Religion of the Semites.* New York:: Appleton.

de Souza, Ronald (1971). "How to Give a Piece of your Mind: Or the Logic of Belief and Assent." *Review of Metaphysics* 25. 52-79.

Sperber, Dan (1968). "Le Structuralisme en Anthropologie." In O. Ducrot et al. *Qu'est-ce que le Structuralisme?.* Paris: Le Seuil.

(1974). "Contre Certains *A priori* Anthropologiques. In Edgar Morin & Massimo Piatelli-Palmarini *L'Unité de l'Homme: Invariants Biologiques et Universaux Culturels.* Paris: Le Seuil. 491-512.

(1975a) *Rethinking Symbolism.* Translated by Alice Morton. Cambridge: Cambridge University Press.

(1975b) "Pourquoi les Animaux Parfaits, les Hybrides et les Monstres Sont-ils Bon à Penser Symboliquement?" *L'Homme* 15 (2). 5-24.

(1980) "Is Symbolic Thought Prerational?" In Mary Foster & Stanley Brandes (eds.) *Symbol as Sense.* New York: Academic Press. 25-44.

(1981). "L'Interpretation en Anthropologie." *L'Homme* 21 (1). 69-82.

Sperber, Dan & Deirdre Wilson (1981). "Irony and the Use-Mention Distinction." In P. Cole (ed.) *Radical Pragmatics.* New York: Academic Press. 295-318.

Thorndyke, Perry W. (1977). "Cognitive Structures in Comprehension and Memory of Narrative Discourse." *Cognitive Psychology* 9. 77-110.

Tornay, Serge (ed.) (1978). *Voir et Nommer les Couleurs.* Nanterre: Laboratoire d'Ethnologie et de Sociologie Comparative.

Triandis, Harry C. et al. (eds.) (1980). *Handbook of Cross-Cultural Psychology.* 6 vol. Boston: Allyn and Bacon.

Untersteiner, Mario (1954). *The Sophists.* Oxford: Blackwell.

Vernant, Jean-Pierre (1955). "Travail et Nature dans la Grèce Ancienne." *Journal de Psychologie.* 1-29.

Vygotsky, Lev S. (1962). *Thought and Language.* Translated by E. Hanfman and G. Vakar. Cambridge Mass.: M.I.T. Press.

Wilson, Brian (ed.) (1970). *Rationality.* Oxford: Blackwell.

Wilson, Edward O. (1975). *Sociobiology: The New Synthesis.* Cambridge, Mass.: Belknap.

(1978). *On Human Nature.* Cambridge, Mass.: Harvard University Press.

References

Young, Michael W. (1979). *The Ethnography of Malinowski*. London: Routledge and Kegan Paul.

Zan, Yigal (1980). *Theoretical and Methodological Foundations for a Scientific Knowledge of Narrative Phenomena*. Ph.D. dissertation: University of California at Los Angeles.

Zegwaard, G.A. (1959). "Headhunting Practices of the Asmat of the Netherlands New Guinea." *American Anthropologist* 61 (1).

Index

Index

Index

CAMBRIDGE STUDIES IN SOCIAL ANTHROPOLOGY

Editor: Jack Goody

Cambridge studies in social anthropology